An American
Child Supreme

THE *CREDO* SERIES

A credo is a statement of belief, an assertion of deep conviction. The *Credo* series offers contemporary American writers whose work emphasizes the natural world and the human community the opportunity to discuss their essential goals, concerns, and practices. Each volume presents an individual writer's *credo,* his or her investigation of what it means to write about human experience and society in the context of the more-than-human world, as well as a biographical profile and complete bibliography of the author's published work. The *Credo* series offers some of our best writers an opportunity to speak to the fluid and subtle issues of rapidly changing technology, social structure, and environmental conditions.

An American
Child Supreme

THE EDUCATION OF A LIBERATION ECOLOGIST

John Nichols

Scott Slovic, *Credo* Series Editor

Credo

MILKWEED EDITIONS

Published 2001 by Milkweed Editions
Printed in Canada
Cover photo of John Nichols on the roof at Mastic taken by David G.
Nichols circa 1946
Cover design by Dale Cooney
Interior photographs courtesy of the author
The text of this book is set in Stone Serif.
01 02 03 04 05   5 4 3 2 1
First Edition

Milkweed Editions, a nonprofit publisher, gratefully acknowledges support from our World As Home funders, the Lila Wallace-Reader's Digest
Fund and Reader's Legacy underwriter Elly Sturgis. Other support has been
provided by the Elmer L. and Eleanor J. Andersen Foundation; Bush
Foundation; Faegre and Benson Foundation; General Mills Foundation;
Marshall Field's Project Imagine with support from the Target Foundation
and Target Stores; McKnight Foundation; Minnesota State Arts Board
through an appropriation by the Minnesota State Legislature and a grant
from the National Endowment for the Arts; Norwest Foundation on
behalf of Norwest Bank Minnesota, Norwest Investment Management
and Trust, Lowry Hill, Norwest Investment Services, Inc.; Lawrence
and Elizabeth Ann O'Shaughnessy Charitable Income Trust in honor of
Lawrence M. O'Shaughnessy; Oswald Family Foundation; Ritz Foundation
on behalf of Mr. and Mrs. E. J. Phelps Jr.; John and Beverly Rollwagen
Fund of the Minneapolis Foundation; St. Paul Companies, Inc.; U.S.
Bancorp Foundation; and generous individuals.

Library of Congress Cataloging-in-Publication Data

Nichols, John Treadwell, 1940–
    An American child supreme : the education of a liberation ecologist /
John Nichols. — 1st ed.
    p.   cm. — (Credo)
    Includes bibliographical references (p.).
    ISBN 1-57131-253-6 (pbk. : alk. paper)
    1. Nichols, John Treadwell, 1940– 2. Authors, American—20th
century—Biography. 3. Economic development—Environmental
aspects. 4. Ecologists—United States—Biography. 5. Human
ecology—Economic aspects. 6. Human ecology in literature.
7. Ecology in literature. 8. Social ecology. 9. Capitalism. I. Title.
II. Credo series (Minneapolis, Minn.)

PS3564.I274 Z463 2001
813'.54—dc21
[B]

                                                        2001016411

This book is printed on acid-free, recycled paper.

To Ruby, Alan, Mike, and Diana

The Nichols family, Taos, New Mexico, 1971: Ruby with Tania and John carrying Luke. *Photo by Justin Locke.*

César Montes and Luis Turcios Lima, leaders of the Guatemalan guerrilla forces, with Alan Howard, 1965. *Courtesy of Alan Howard.*

Alan Howard and Mike Kimmel, 1982. *Photo by John Nichols.*

Nichols with Diana Oughton, Chichicastenango, Guatemala, 1964. *Photo by Tim Weld.*

An American Child Supreme

All I know is that my happiness is built on the misery of other people, so that I eat because others go hungry, that I am clothed when other people go almost naked through the frozen cities in winter; and that fact poisons me, disturbs my serenity, makes me write propaganda when I would rather play. . . .

—John Reed, author of *Ten Days That Shook the World*

An American
Child Supreme

An American Child Supreme

THE EDUCATION OF A LIBERATION ECOLOGIST

by John Nichols

It's a mystery to me how anybody among us develops a social conscience. We are raised in a so-called democracy whose Declaration of Independence informs us that all men are created equal. But our economic system is predicated on ruthless competition that trains most everybody, including writers, to be relatively heartless predators. A majority of us blithely accepts the inequalities that define the system, even though, in our more reflective moments, we understand that our attitudes and our lifestyles are driving the system toward an environmental apocalypse increasingly ordained as all the elements of our consumptive folly merge into a single overriding catastrophe. When I say "environmental" I mean human community as well as everything else. *All* life on earth is natural, no exceptions.

Today I am told repeatedly by shrill voices on the "lunatic fringe" of the media and the environmental

3

movement that these are the worst of times. That may be true. Yet during the first five years of my life, which began on July 23, 1940, close to sixty million people were murdered worldwide, and the manufacturing capacity of much of the "civilized" world was bombed until the gears ceased to mesh, even the grandest of wheels stopped turning, and most of the cities that housed the apparatus lay in rubble. By the time of my fifth birthday the planet was a graveyard and an environmental disaster. To emphasize the point, my nation incinerated the people of Hiroshima and Nagasaki with atomic weapons.

During those five years I lost my French mother, Monique Le Braz, to endocarditis (in 1942) and my father temporarily to the Pacific campaign, where he spent time in the Solomon Islands, Okinawa, then China. When he returned from overseas he was married again, and the three of us set about to construct a civilian life in a postwar boom era that would grow fat on the Marshall Plan and other reconstruction juggernauts aiding the conquered nations. That climax consumerism eventually segued directly into the ecodisaster facing us today. My father, the veteran, was so gun-shy that I was forbidden to own a cap pistol, even though my heroes in 1946 and 1947 were among America's favorite gunslingers: Roy Rogers, Gene Autry, and Hopalong Cassidy. On Easter Day 1947, my parents finally relented and gave me the desired six-shooter. They felt sorry for me because I was laid up with the mumps. Shortly thereafter I caught my dad by surprise, firing a jolly round of caps behind his back when he least expected the attack. He swiveled instantly and knocked me across the room, which was a wakeup call of sorts.

War (including cold war), and the relentless preparation for it, was a major foundation of the eco-apocalypse that has been fashioned during my life-time. The only way to avoid war is for people to treat each other as equals. The socioeconomics of such an equality would be a great blessing for the "natural" world.

Of course, my liberal parents did not consciously raise me to be a bigot, a greedy consumer, a war-monger, or a fanatical environmental parasite. But they came from the North American middle class that by default perpetuated those values at a time when our victorious nation was gearing up for a bout with untrammeled prosperity. Fortunately for me, my father and his dad were also professional naturalists who gave me a curiosity about beetles, lizards, and herring gulls that would eventually cause me to pause when I considered, from a more in-depth perspec-tive, the spending habits of my fellow Americans.

The creed underlying their brand of naturalist could best be summed up in a statement by John Muir: "When we try to pick out anything by itself, we find it hitched to everything else in the universe." The inference is that we must develop a macroscopic overview of life in order to both understand and solve our problems. From an early age, I had the good luck to be influenced in this direction.

My most powerful memories of early childhood derive from life at my grandparents' summer home at Mastic, on the south shore of Long Island. The house was an old colonial number built by the father of our direct ancestor, William Floyd, who signed the Declaration of Independence for New York State. The house was surrounded by over six hundred acres of wild forest and saltwater marshes. Even the non-naturalist grown-ups around me were interested in turtles, herons, and butterflies. My father collected mice and other small mammals for the American Museum of Natural History in New York City, and I often followed him on his trapping rounds, pouching the little critters. My grandfather (and namesake), John T. Nichols, was curator of recent fishes at the museum and a significant ornithologist. As a boy I often visited his office, where I ogled shelves of pickled frogs, salamanders, and sticklebacks lodged among old briar pipes and dented fedoras.

So from the start I was encouraged to marvel at living organisms with more than the usual amateur enthusiasm. On July evenings, family members sat very still on the Mastic veranda listening, with an almost rapturous intellectual serenity, to whippoor-wills beyond the lawn. I don't think any of these people penned shrill tracts against the environmental and social devastation caused by the surge of post-war capitalism that soon dominated American life, but they gave me a love of towering woodcocks, praying mantis eggs, and monarch caterpillars munching milkweed leaves. Their ecosympathies were basically proletarian and made me aware of alternatives to our nihilistic lust for prosperity. To be a true nature lover, you must question the status quo that destroys nature at every turn. I have always blessed my family for laying that groundwork.

My father liked comforts, but in his checkered career as a businessman, a CIA spook, a student, and a professor of psychology, he never went after the gelt: we lived a pretty simple life. Far more interesting to my dad were the behavioral patterns of mourning doves that could give insight into human aggression, insight that might one day help lead to peaceful solutions of human conflict. Pop was a compassionate man with a sense of biological proportions, appalled by his own angers and, particularly in his later years, dismayed by our collapsing ecosystem. Please keep in mind that ecosystem means inner-city Philadelphia as well as Glacier National Park. A hopeful future requires that we develop a "social ecology."

"The trouble with me," my dad once said, "is that I was brought up to believe in a stability of existence that just doesn't exist." He understood that that hypothetical stability is the central prevarication driving most Americans in their hopeless pursuit of lucre, equity, *things*. He also knew that the more we consume, eager to be "secure," the more we undermine every level of resource and community that sustains us.

Pop was born in the William Floyd house at Mastic in 1916 and he returned there often during his chaotic life that had been deeply traumatized by his young wife's death and a world war. I vaguely remember his protests when the Suffolk County Mosquito Commission saturated Mastic with DDT in the late 1940s, rubbing out many mosquitoes, bumblebees, songbirds, and other life-forms on the place. Fields and forests were butchered to make people "comfortable" and "secure." For a family of naturalists that must have seemed a nasty bit of senseless doggerel from the miracle of postwar technology— "stability" indeed.

I don't recall anyone in my immediate (childhood) family fighting for civil rights. Probably my parents voted for Ike and Dick. My grandmother, Cornelia Floyd Nichols, had a couple of low-key servants at her summer place and admitted to me in my early manhood that she was a racist and "too old to change." Grammie certainly did not wear this prejudice as a badge of honor on her sleeve, but she was directly descended from the Signer, William Floyd, who had also held slaves. Such contradictions run counter to my family's ethical and naturalist traditions and, to some extent, render those traditions neutral. Similar contradictions are the central tragedy of our nation, where there is a vast difference between the destructive capitalism that drives us and our democratic ideals.

During the 1950s, when my dad worked for the

CIA, he did not tiptoe around in a trenchcoat and black hat casting anticommunist broadsides against the evil empire of Soviet expansionism. Yet in papers I found after his death, he mentioned that his job was to keep "the communists from taking over the complete direction of our lives." He believed force was needed to deter force. And he likened super-power politics to scientific explanations of life: "For matter to exist the free flow of energy must be im-peded." As a cold war scientist, he hoped to control the arms race so that Armageddon could be avoided at all costs. He believed that secrecy helped maintain human confidence in "détente," a false stability like the one that had characterized his childhood. At the same time, he understood that every penny we spent for atomic weapons as "protection" triggered similar expenditures (and paranoia) in the Soviet Union, making us increasingly less secure. "The trouble with empirical science," he once told me, "is that scien-tists pretend make-believe is unreal." Dad must have realized the contradictions inherent in his own job were untenable.

Later, when he became a psychology professor most interested in achieving world peace by under-standing the communication of human emotions, Pop's message demanded the need for social respon-sibility. That had always been an important compo-nent of his naturalist's creed.

Neither my father, mother, nor grandparents had much serious interest in sports. But because I date one of my first important steps toward egalitarian beliefs to an incident (triggered by an athletic contest) that occurred in second grade at my Westbury (Long Island) elementary school, I must dwell a bit on sports. A kid named Emerick Tedesky walked up to me and asked if I was rooting for the Yankees or the Dodgers in the World Series. This had to be October 1947. Ignorant of baseball (and all other sports, for that matter) but not wishing to seem stupid, I replied, "The Dodgers." Emerick Tedesky punched me in the nose and I went down like Bambi on ice, thoroughly befuddled. But when I regained my feet, my life had been transformed. I wanted revenge, of course; but I also hated the Yankees; and I was a Dodger fan for life. A week later, catching Emerick by surprise, I shoved him down the schoolyard steps, giving him a bloody nose.

In 1947 the Yankees had already long been considered a monolith, and the Brooklyn Dodgers were a talented but bumbling team. They also had Jackie Robinson up for his initial year in the bigs, and he became my first and most enduring sports hero. I don't know if Emerick Tedesky hated the Dodgers (and had punched me) because the Brooklyns were playing a Negro, but that may have been one of the subliminal messages imparted to me by his mean little fist. In any case, his blow made the world a much more complicated place, and it also opened up a universe of fabulous adventure. Within moments I had developed interests in hockey and football also, rooting for the New York Rangers and the Giants; and I began to read line scores and collect baseball cards with downright venomous intensity. Getting smacked in the face gave me heroes like Roy Campanella and Don Newcombe, as well as Pee Wee Reese and Maurice Richard. With one punch that obstreperous kid had propelled me toward integration.

I have witnessed with heartbreak all the racial conflict in sports subsequent to my rude 1947 initiation, and one thing I do believe: Emerick Tedesky helped to cast my fate with the wretched of the earth. Be reminded that ozone, elephants, and hummingbirds, as well as Rwandans and migrant workers, are to be included in that category.

My father spoke Russian and French. My maternal grandmother, Maggie Robert Le Braz—"Mamita"—a French resident of Barcelona, spoke French, English, and Spanish. Unfortunately, after my mother died (and until I reached the age of twenty), I could not visit relatives in Europe because of a conflict between the U.S. and European sides of the family. Nevertheless, aware of my origins and intrigued by my father's linguistic skills, I was as fascinated at an early age by foreign languages and other cultures as I was bewitched by small mammals and pickled fishes. My father played exuberant guitar and sang Russian and French folk tunes as well as classic English ballads and cowboy melodies. I began a collection of foreign newspapers. Relatives who'd been abroad sent them to me. With saved allowances I purchased French, Spanish, and Portuguese blats at New York's foreign newsstands. Though unable to read them, I was a fanatic little manic-obsessive and pored over those newspapers, which were among my most precious possessions. I spent hours absorbed by a Dick Tracy comic strip in Arabic. Once, when I was twelve years old, I bought a thick paperback that promised to teach me German through pictures. From a clever assortment of cartoon stick figures at work and at play I taught myself to say: "Das ist die braun hut. Die braun hut ist auf meinen knie." I wanted to speak multiple languages like my dad and my French grandmother and ultimately I succeeded, although not until after college. But very early on I had the *desire* for these complex linguistic connections to everything else in the universe.

My French grandmother, Mamita, was the daughter of a well-known writer from Brittany, Anatole Le Braz—my maternal great-grandfather. Anatole Le Braz wrote books about Breton culture, some of which are still in print eighty years after his death. Most Brittany towns have an Anatole Le Braz street or place or some small plaque recognizing the importance of his work. Not until the summer of 1960, when I finally visited my grandmother in Barcelona, did I receive the gift from her of a book by Anatole. The paperback was a precious introduction to my foreign identity, albeit an unreadable one at the time. That his literature spoke of a people often at odds with, and subjugated by, the dominant French regimes escaped me then but would grow in importance later. My great-grandfather was a bourgeois and by no stretch a revolutionary, but his work speaks for the underdogs.

Anatole Le Braz had three wives: the first two died on him without a breath of scandal involved. His final helpmate was an American woman, Mary Davison, whose brother, H. P. Davison, a business partner of J. P. Morgan, had—to put it politely—an elaborate mansion at Peacock Point on the north shore of Long Island near Locust Valley. The Davison family was prominent in Republican politics, and H. P.'s son, Trubee, did a stint as president of the American Museum of Natural History in Manhattan. He got my mother a job at the museum, and that's where my father and Monique met. Because Anatole Le Braz had been married to Mary Davison, whenever Mamita visited America after Monique's death she stayed at Peacock Point. I was sometimes allowed to visit there like a child from a Dickensian blacking factory on holiday at the Taj Mahal. We are speaking here of a baroque mansion, located on Long Island Sound, with its own internal telephone exchange, elevators, indoor and outdoor tennis courts, stables, elaborate lawns, gardens, gazebos, croquet playing fields, and a fleet of chauffeured station wagons. Over fifty servants were on hand to coddle the socialites and politicos. Mamita—who herself had "only" three servants in a modest Barcelona apartment—was ecstatic at Peacock Point. During my first visits there I was held in big-time thrall by the fairy tale. But some time after the Emerick Tedesky incident, I developed an attitude about Peacock Point, embarrassed by such conspicuous consumption and by the servants' role in it, too.

It made me uncomfortable to be waited on. Often twenty or more family members chowed down at Sunday luncheon in the Big House, presided over by my great-aunt Kate, also known as Goggie (the widow of H. P. Davison). All kinds of waiters and waitresses, led by the head butler, Frederick, deferentially passed out the finger bowls and the sorbets between courses. It soon became my habit, when I arrived at Peacock Point, to burst into the bustling kitchen where noisy servants treated me with a kind of boffo joviality. I suppose I wanted to mollify them—with my friendly gestures and by crossing into *their* world—for having to wait on me in such humiliating formal circumstances on the other side of the kitchen door. Then I dashed off to hit tennis balls with a stable boy on the grass court beside the swimming pool.

So I believe that on my father's side of the family, the narrowing of social purview created by privilege was offset by the naturalist proclivities of Mastic's owners, and also by their historical roots. It is important to me that my great-(times five)-grandfather, William Floyd, signed the Declaration of Independence for New York State. This document is a revolutionary credo whose most memorable sentiments were translated almost verbatim in 1945 by Ho Chi Minh to begin the Vietnamese declaration of independence as well. In my family, roots were paramount and daily evident at Mastic dating back to the early 1700s. My stepmother's Gleason family from Vermont was educated, vigorously aware, and widely connected to its origins also. Anatole Le Braz and his heirs took care of that sort of continuity on the other side of the pond. I will mention also that my great-aunt Susan Nichols Pulsifer, my namesake's sister, once wrote a book of family history called *The Witch's Breed,* tracing the Nichols side of my dad's people back to an ancestor, Susanna Martin, who, after an unfair trial in 1692, was hanged for being a witch in Salem, Massachusetts. A transcript of that procedure, still extant, indicates she was condemned largely for being a feminist several centuries before Betty Friedan reared her insistent head.

My connection to that sort of history is not to be sneezed at. I suppose it could have molded me into an unbearable snob, but I think instead it became an important part of the macroscopic overview that made me almost fanatically conscious and proud of being an American. Were we all so well documented, maybe everybody would become a revolutionary social ecologist. When you hail from a family that acknowledges its own history as mine does, you are prone at least to believe in the *rights* of history for others and for the land. Perhaps that is a reason I ultimately wound up in Taos, New Mexico, where many of my Native American friends inhabit terrain and dwellings that have been in their families for centuries, and the Chicano community across the valley irrigates its fields from acequias built by direct ancestors three hundred years ago.

My father entered the CIA during the Korean War in 1951. While he spent many months in Alaska "monitoring Russian broadcasts," my mother, two brothers, and I festered cheerfully in Wilton, Connecticut. Eventually we headed with Pop for rural Virginia, driving through a deserted Washington, D.C., at 2:00 A.M. on the January 1953 night after Eisenhower's inauguration. Colvin Run was a tiny town on a Route 7 highway spur about forty minutes west of Washington. There were two general stores and a grange hall, period. We rented a nice house on a couple of acres in dairy farm country. Northern Virginia was rural, then, and it was segregated. I went to the all-white Forestville Elementary School and attended eighth grade in the white-only Herndon High School. Although black people were all around us, I almost never saw them.

One man by the name of Harv used to show up on the grange hall steps across from our general store. There he waited. The store had everything: homemade ice cream, penny candy, OshKosh B'Gosh overalls, bread, and vegetables. Sorry, however: no Negroes allowed inside. In fact, the owners often slipped segregation pamphlets into my grocery bags, and I studied them carefully: I was twelve years old.

Harv waited patiently on the grange hall steps for a white person to come along and buy him things in that establishment. "I am the child of a slave," he told me. Harv had white hair, few teeth, and spoke real slow. The store owners' daughter, who suffered from cerebral palsy, often lay in a crib in the store. Her parents loved and cared for her; in that respect they were both an inspiration. Also, they sure were good to me. But the segregation pamphlets they handed out were venom at its worst. And you can bet, no matter *what* document had been signed long ago by William Floyd, that Harv never did set foot inside their wonderful store.

Our garbage man was black. Once a week he picked up the trash in his old truck and hauled it away. A day came when Mother lost her engagement ring and frantically reached the conclusion that it must have fallen into the kitchen wastebasket moments before I emptied it outside on collection day. So we drove to the collector's house. Picture an unpainted and weathered wooden home whose windows lacked panes of glass. The porch was lopsided, and we could see under the house because it was raised on short stilts, delta style. A man, a woman dressed in rags, and some barefoot kids gathered on the porch, astonished to see white folks arriving in a big Buick. All around the house, dwarfing it, framing it, damn near *ingesting* it, were mountains of garbage, heaps of trash, festering mounds of refuse.

It could be this part of my story is apocryphal: Mother and I got out and were ushered to a spot in one pile where we dug around feverishly, searching for the engagement ring, while those flabbergasted

17 ✎

people watched. If somebody had taken a photograph and sent it to Norman Rockwell, I wonder could he have done it justice?

I remember *Whites Only* signs in Virginia restaurant windows, segregated drinking fountains, the "colored" balconies of movie theaters. Boy Scouts were lily white, and our friends 100 percent Anglo-American. Toward the end of my eighth grade year at Herndon High (in the spring of 1954), *Brown v. Board of Education* became the law, desegregating our nation's schools. Next day my friends showed up on campus toting baseball bats, tire chains, brass knuckles, and a simple but ingenious weapon: potatoes with razor blades imbedded in one side to be thrown at Negroes if they dared to integrate. I neither participated nor protested: I observed and avoided confrontation. But I think I was beginning to feel that life was gonna get complicated.

At the age of twelve I began working summers for a gentleman farmer friend of the family, Goodwin Locke. That's when my writing career commenced. On his lush piece of land this dear man grew tomatoes, asparagus, raspberries, and mushrooms. A large spick-and-span chicken coop supported an egg operation. We candled the eggs in a basement and caponized young chickens using a large hypodermic needle to inject a white hormone pill into the loose, scruffy neck skin of male birds. I spent long hours with a pressurized cannister of nicotine poison strapped to my back, spraying the raspberries for aphids with a solution that, improperly diluted, could have wiped out a fair-sized metropolis. We delivered our toxic produce to fancy Arlington and Washington restaurants.

During lunch breaks on the farm, Goodwin and I lounged in his wide Mexican hammock reading Damon Runyon's New York gangster stories to each other: my favorite was "Johnny One Eye." And Damon Runyon knocked my socks off. His slangy, comical criminals captured my imagination and made me want to rob banks, bet on the ponies, and eat gefilte fish. Those characters were so *irreverent,* and they inspired me to begin writing wiseapple, slang-laden, and humorous short stories myself. Most of my characters inhabited the underworld; very few were middle class; all of them carried "pizzalovers." It seems I was on to something.

My allowance of a quarter a week stopped when I started working. Now I was responsible for buying my own clothes. The summer (of 1955) after my first year at a Connecticut prep school, Loomis, I worked for a big florist in McLean, Virginia, weeding, steaming the flower beds of enormous greenhouses, transplanting seedlings outside. My fellow workers were poor, animated, friendly. For lunch we were invited inside the owner's house where his wife fed us five-course meals, complete with biscuits and gravy. Her egalitarian generosity made an indelible impression on me.

Private school is a privilege extended largely to the ruling class, but my situation was interesting. In later years my father claimed that I was sent to escape our family's disjointed emotional politics. Because we were relatively "poor," my dad's sister took care of tuition; I paid for my clothes and most everything else. Always I was broke and slouched around, begging pennies off my classmates. Academically I floundered, yet I published stories and articles in the school newspaper and literary magazine, and athletics saved my life. I was embarrassed by privilege, resented boys with money, and played hockey like a Neanderthal. Too, I hated the rigid authority, which echoed a rigidity at home. But away from home I was suddenly not afraid to talk back, and a lot of pent-up anger burst. Granted, we all rebel at that age. But I was a loose cannon with a pretty well-oiled self-destruct mechanism.

During my first two years in gaol I constantly mouthed off at professors, arrived late to classes, refused to clean my room for inspection, fought with other students, led nighttime raids on neighboring dormitories, cut morning chapel because church bored me, failed French and algebra (twice), violated dress codes, cursed vehemently and used gangster slang, and let my hair grow too long. I was obnoxious, outgoing, blunt, loud mouthed, happy-go-lucky, and, given that I was lacking even rudimentary survival artifice, rather stupid.

Accordingly, I spent all my free time locked in punitive study halls. What they never discovered was that I had in my possession a .25 caliber semi-automatic pistol (stolen from my grandmother's attic) and a Harrington and Richardson 12-gauge shotgun (a *serious* no-no). When the devil urged me on, friends and I would stand on the banks of the nearby Connecticut River, and, while the Loomis clock loudly (and exhaustively) chimed the quarter hour, we blasted sodapop cans in the water.

Obviously, I wanted to rebel. I really yearned to be free of constraints, free to speak for myself. To hell with the hypocrisy of social conventions. My father once wrote, "Civilization is based on restraint; evolution and change is based on non-restraint." My instincts toward nonrestraint at Loomis were many, but my learning curve had been atrophied by Puritan brainwashing. Into the breach stepped rock 'n' roll, eager to get the ball of my rebellion rolling faster.

When Little Richard, Chuck Berry, Elvis Presley, Fats Domino, and their noisy ilk took over the music scene, I went ballistic. Me and all the rest of us moral midget white kids destined to become doctors, lawyers, and stockbrokers. Maybe the music excited me more, however; for starters, I promptly learned to play guitar. And immediately gravitated to the roots of it all, the blues. That meant Leadbelly singing "Goodnight, Irene" and the Josh White version of "Jelly." Other influences were Champion Jack Dupree and Brownie McGee and Sonny Terry, who led me right into the folk music scene, a snake that soon enough proffered the evil apple of pinko crooners like Woody Guthrie and Pete Seeger. They had political axes to grind that protested *against* pollution as well as *for* union wages. The music I came to love acknowledged, celebrated, or lobbied on behalf of, the downtrodden and the environment. It was working class, green, and seditious.

Whenever I put together a small stake, I bought records. Broke, I sold them. During my protracted adolescence no sweeter thrill existed than that first loud downstroke on my ancient Gibson at the start of "Blue Suede Shoes": "Well, it's a one for the money . . ." And there were Alan Lomax books to read, and lives to learn about belonging to Jelly Roll Morton, Blind Lemon Jefferson, Billie Holiday. How anybody could listen to their stuff without seriously questioning the status quo is a mystery to me. Music is *powerful*.

By the end of my sophomore year at Loomis I had flunked French and algebra. I was actually kicked out of school for behavioral reasons but then allowed to continue when I won a student council election as a write-in candidate. I arrived home in Virginia just as my father initiated proceedings for a bitter divorce and our family collapsed. Uh-oh, Spaghetti-O. It became clear to me in about thirty seconds that there is no stability on earth, particularly if you depend on dysfunctional relatives to provide it for you. Fearful of being set adrift, I made a conscious decision to tow the line at Loomis, a simple survival tactic and a fairly cynical act, given my budding rebellious worldview. When I returned to school for my junior year I sucked in my gut, began modestly brownnosing the status quo, and my life became immeasureably easier. Fawning isn't pretty, but occasionally it promotes longevity.

During the summer between my junior and senior years at Loomis I took a Greyhound out west and spent a week in Taos, New Mexico, helping Justin Locke, the brother of Goodwin (my Virginia employer), replaster an adobe wall on his property, clean irrigation ditches, and empty a bottle of mescal to get at the worm on the bottom. The Taos Pueblo turned me on: so did the ancient (and famous) Ranchos church and the rustic beauty of small irrigated fields below Justin's house. Everything was so *different,* including the population of Spanish speakers who seemed linked to my mother's roots, to Mamita in Barcelona, and to my new hero, Ernest Hemingway (who made me want to write, learn Spanish, fight bulls, and win the Nobel Prize).

My next step that summer took me to Portal, Arizona, where, thanks to a letter of introduction from my grandfather (the ichthyologist), I worked for room and board at an American Museum of Natural History research station. I helped scientists collect lizards, rattlesnakes, and gloriosa beetles in a magnificent wild country. But my summer really shifted into high gear when I fought forest fires in the Chiricahua Mountains alongside a group of Chicanos from Rodeo, New Mexico, and several Mexican nationals. Pedro, the ringleader of our unruly gang, had only one arm; Turkey, the cook, once slapped a scorpion crawling up my thigh. Our straw boss, a racist, anglo, ex–rodeo cowboy, treated the Latinos with patronizing scorn. I resisted being linked to him simply because of race (and class), siding with the majority in a situation that at one point came dangerously close to mutiny. That was one of the first times I mustered enough courage to physically draw the line on behalf of underdogs . . . in order to save my own skin.

Between fires, on R and R excursions to the red-light district of Agua Prieta (opposite Douglas, Arizona), tall, thin, mournful Frank, who spoke not a word of English, kept me amused—and a virgin—while our buddies went nuts screwing *putas* in claustrophobic cubicles behind the bar.

Returning home at 3:00 A.M. dead drunk in the back of Pedro's pickup hoarsely bawling "Cielito Lindo" with those hail fellows under the glitter of myriad stars was a grand occasion for a boy like me. Back east, just for fun, I wrote a novella called *The Journey,* which drew heavily from indigenous culture, southwestern landscape, and growing sympathies for the poor. Steinbeck and Hemingway played their heavy hands across my style, with *Old Man and the Sea* and *The Grapes of Wrath* ever present. Tom Lea's *Wonderful Country* mopped up whatever they had missed.

Never underestimate the power of literature. "Hungry man, reach for the book: it is a weapon," said Bertolt Brecht. Nelson Algren put it this way: "I submit that literature is made upon any occasion that a challenge is put to the legal apparatus by a conscience in touch with humanity."

My novella also rejected God.

You could say that I was gravitating toward class betrayal, though that may be an overly dramatic (and self-conscious) assessment conjured strictly for the purposes of this essay. But I was on the scent, romantically enamored of the working class, chafing at the "unfair" world. Instinctively, I must have desired liberation from the repressed sand traps of my own family and culture, though I had no concept of poverty's damnation. Spanish was an exciting "peasant" tongue . . . and also one of my mom's inherent lingos, as she had lived for years in Spain. Surely I yearned to delve into a more "earthy" (and liberated, I thought) culture than my own.

One book I specifically remember being taught at Loomis was Joseph Conrad's *Victory*. The message of the novel that made an impression on me was that you cannot remain detached in life because the outside world will come in and destroy you anyway. You cannot, as the main protagonist Axel Heyst's father counseled, "Look on—make no sound," and expect to escape from the gory realities. I've probably garbled the message, but the garble resonated in me for years, caught as I was in my own personal contradiction of fearing confrontation while pining to liberate myself, a gesture that almost always requires battle. What I finally learned, the hard way, was that concentrated efforts to steer clear of trouble were often more destructive than just joining the fray. Cleverly, I nourished my writing as a way for a timid soul to be bold despite himself.

(Thus did the starving anarchist bide his time, crouching in a tawdry garret penning shrill tracts with his goose quill while manufacturing crude saltpeter bombs!)

Toward the end of my senior year at Loomis I asked a friend to help me study for a chemistry final exam. I was flunking the course and might not graduate. My pal refused, explaining that it was nothing personal, but if I did well on the test that would lower his place on the curve. This rejection has dogged me all my life in a way that explains the universe. I flunked chemistry and had to be voted through at graduation by a faculty committee. I believe my rank in a class of seventy-two boys was sixty-ninth. I stumbled out of those hallowed portals breathing a heartfelt sigh of relief, incredulous that I had survived.

Yes, I had been accepted at a summer ice hockey school in Moose Jaw, Saskatchewan; but my hormones were lit up like a Christmas tree, so I chose instead to hover near my Hartford girlfriend before entering Hamilton College in upstate New York that fall. Good luck found me a dishwashing job at the Maple Hill Restaurant of West Hartford. I rented a room at the downtown YMCA where, every night before bed, in the communal bathroom as I brushed my teeth, older gay men assessed and propositioned me but never essayed a physical assault. Most afternoons were spent with my girl at her house making out like bandits until 4:00 P.M., when she dropped me off at my job, which lasted until midnight. My dishroom coworkers were a small, rugged Czech immigrant and a delicate, noisy Puerto Rican. The Czech had a large family and two other jobs; he never, *ever* complained. The Puerto Rican laughed a lot. We rarely had time for serious kidding around, yet I felt like a man and joyously free. After closing, I ground all the kitchen griddles and cleaned and flushed the grease bins, if necessary. Then I helped an old guy mop the acres of linoleum.

What was his name? Maybe Charles. Very carefully, Charles explained how to mop the floor like a professional. Forget the restaurant's owners, who often treated us badly and paid low wages; the job was important of itself.

"You diminish yourself," Charles said, "if you do a job, no matter what the situation, less than the best you can."

This was *not* a cliché. A severe critic, Charles checked out my mopping carefully. He was tall and tired with a quiet, wistful demeanor, but I listened to this black man well. Since that time, I have separated the personal insults flung by rote into most work from my personal need to do well no matter what the situation. Not always an easy task, given that insults and hassles are built into the profit-making apparatus in order to keep workers "in their place." I have long hated the fact that most tasks which are the backbone of a viable society are dishonored by our culture and rewarded poorly so that the owners of the production apparatus may reap unseemly rewards.

"Strange Fruit" is one of Billie Holiday's signature tunes. At seventeen I learned it off a Josh White record and used to sing it with a great deal of angry feeling against the racism it describes. Two years after I memorized the song—during my sophomore season at Hamilton—I wrote a novel about segregation called *Don't Be Forlorn*. Recently I retrieved from my downtown Taos storage locker that novel that I wrote, then put aside at nineteen. And I reread it (or I should say painfully skimmed it) for the first time in forty years.

The plot of *Don't Be Forlorn* is seriously warped by the weight of catastrophically maudlin writing. Mawkish stereotypes and an absolute lack of subtlety abound on both sides of the race question; my writing is outlandishly melodramatic. I don't think bad literature makes one a racist, but it sure is embarrassing. I wrote the novel not for a class, nor for a literary magazine, but simply to satisfy my own curiosity.

The book begins with an epigraph, identified as a stanza from a Negro folk song:

> Hush mah babe, don' be forlorn
> 'cause you was lynched 'fore you was born.
> Your skin is black, an' dey wan' it understood,
> Though you is one day old, you is no damn
>   good.

The story obviously derives from the 1955 lynching of Emmett Till. In my novel, while visiting his grandparents in a small southern town, a teenage Negro from the North argues with a white girl in a drugstore. She tells her husband, who, with a friend, kidnaps and murders the northern boy. The local sheriff, a cartoon Sheriff Rainey type well before the real Sheriff Rainey had made national news, hires a broken-down, alcoholic cartoon white lawyer to prosecute the two white men arrested for the crime. The sheriff knows his ineffectual lawbooks will bungle the case, allowing the accused to go free. Predictably, an all-white jury abets this travesty, and the murderers are declared innocent. During the trial the spastic lawyer's cartoon wife berates him for taking the case. And, for a bit of irony, ludicrous cartoon black kids spouting "whuffo shonuff" dialect outside the courthouse get rich selling lemonade.

No congratulations are in order simply because the injustice depicted in my novel was, and still is, a matter of national fact. Ten paragraphs into the clumsy jeremiad I am sure that any black citizen of America would want to lynch *me* for committing racist buffoonery. But my story does indicate a desire for social justice. One page touches on the brutality of "free" enterprise; another angrily explains why, in a county 63 percent black, not a single registered black voter is able to qualify for a jury. Also, there is a passionate description of a guitarist singing the blues while the drunken white lawyer sympathizes desperately with the musician and his message. Though completely unsuited for the task, I labored fretfully to depict the horrors of segregation.

A word about religion. I was baptized Catholic, and, after my birth mother's death, Pa and New Ma raised me Episcopalian. We went to services every Sunday, I attended Sunday school, I learned all the hymns and recitations. I said my prayers at night and could launch a proper grace at table for the grandparents when asked. Loomis forced me to chapel every morning before classes and to church on Sunday, soporifics more effective than phenobarbital. Freshmen and sophomores at Hamilton were required at Sunday chapel, where I think attendance was taken; juniors and seniors were excused. The moment I had that choice I availed myself of it with a vengeance, rarely darkening a Christian edifice again for reasons other than a Halloween prank or a friend's or family member's funeral.

Religion made little sense and just plain never took. I didn't like horror movies or basketball either. Despite the routine efforts to convert me, I never believed in God; I never bought into the fear or the guilt or the genuflection. I *did* understand that belief, however abstract or based on hocus-pocus, was real and could move people to fainting, ecstasy, irrational behavior. But thinking humans thus motivated by heaven or hell or that elaborate fairy tale, the Bible, were bizarre and untrustworthy in my eyes, like movies viewed through 3-D glasses. And the tons of literature I read or was force-fed that carried on about questions of faith left me puzzled, uninvolved, and with a dislocated jaw from yawning. My only faith has turned out to be the veneration of life.

Is atheism *necessary* for a social conscience? I don't know, but maybe it helps. We have to shuck off so many restrictions and prejudices in order to *think*. Our anthropocentric deity (created by Man in His own image) seems to be a barrier to creative and humanistic evolution. Too many theology-driven commandments justifying conquest or the accumulation of lucre have paved the way to environmental (and social) ruin.

In 1983, I spoke with liberation theologists in Nicaragua who had a radical commitment to the poor. I also have dear pals who wear the cloth. And because so many friends of mine are believers, I generally stay mum on the subject. This has been more of a survival tactic than tactful, and I've resented my timidity. Our need for "meaning" and "immortality" seem to deflect us from squarely facing the prosaic realities of routine aliveness. Belief in afterlife is like believing that space colonization (another impossible abstraction) will save us when we destroy the planet. Certainly the human-oriented nature of most religious belief deflects humanity away from a visceral reverence for the "natural" environment. Is this a fatal mistake?

At Hamilton, following my reformation at Loomis, I did not make waves. I was a good athlete, gregarious, funny, socially adept, and ubiquitous in friendships and interests. I did not challenge the ruling apparatus or reveal my dark side. Consequently, I was popular. Each year I was voted into my class's honor society, and during my junior and senior years I also served on the Honor Court, a body of elected students (guided by faculty advisors) that enforced the college's honor code. We held trials, and upperclassmen found guilty of cheating were thrown out of school for good; freshmen could return after a year's suspension. Our proceedings went smoothly until a basketball cocaptain fell afoul of our judgments; we expelled him without reprieve, according to the law. However, in review our faculty committee balked: the kid was too important to expel. Why? Because alumni coughed when the college teams excelled. We student members of the Honor Court, incensed by the faculty's duplicity, threatened to resign. A compromise ensued; though an upperclassman, the guilty boy was allowed to return after his suspension. I felt betrayed because every student, on entering Hamilton, was required to sign the honor code and abide by its regulations, which pointedly allowed no exceptions to the rule.

Another of my powerful learning experiences was tied to Hamilton's policy on fraternities. Because the college lacked facilities to house and feed most upperclassmen, it needed the campus Greek houses to fill those needs. Hence, the administration guaranteed to every incoming freshman at least one bid.

This was known as a system of "100 percent opportunity." In practice, here's how it worked. After rushing, but before the bids were tendered, representatives from each house met with a faculty committee to divvy up the geeks nobody wanted. That gathering was known as the Pig Pool. As the duly elected representative from my house—Theta Delta Chi—I negotiated with other fraternities at the Pig Pool over who would extend bids to which outcasts in order to implement 100 percent opportunity. The infighting among us slave traders was fierce, ugly, humiliating. Representatives bickered and wheeled and dealed. Afterward, at Theta Delt, I delivered a report on the "pigs" to whom we must now extend bids. The brothers complained that this pig had pimples, that one was a Jew, another guy had horrible BO. Lamely, I tried to sell the potential pledges by pointing out that their fathers were rich, or they had earned straight A's in high school, or they were excellent chess players.

Unfortunately, any pig, thus forcibly thrust upon the fraternity against its will, was usually hazed unmercifully by the brothers until eventually he might quit in dismay, while college officials, the architects of 100 percent opportunity, looked the other way. It is a mark of my cowardice/cynicism/survival instinct that I went along with the system, which paralleled that of racism in the South. Given my stature at Hamilton, if I'd quit the fraternity indignantly my action might have had important repercussions. But

I kept my mouth shut, played some obscene Oscar Brand tunes on my guitar, and drank a lot of milk punch on Sunday morning of house parties.

My generation was called the Silent Generation. We came of age in the fifties. Perhaps our silence was a reflexive clamming up in reaction to the anticommunist spell cast by Joe McCarthy. On the other hand, maybe our silence was less a way to avoid stumbling into condemnation than it was a self-serving attempt to let that oppressive nature take its course so long as we ourselves (white, middle class, educated) were blessed. I don't think Georgia tenant farmers or hod carriers from Harlem were part of the Silent Generation. That mantle was carried more comfortably by us boys from Loomis and Deerfield, Hamilton and Dartmouth—the future ruling class.

On the other hand, my best friend at Hamilton did not fit this mold, and to that I owe a great deal in my life. His name was (still is!) Alan Howard. During my last two years at school we were very close and shared many zany adventures. Alan had the grown-up, analytical (and political) mind, and I was sort of an idealistic, immature bozo much given to literary hyperbole. We acted in a play together, started an oafish comic greeting card company, and wallowed together in Thomas Wolfe, Ernest Hemingway, and F. Scott Fitzgerald. I think my gift to Alan was to lure (or perhaps goad) him toward aesthetic pursuits: poetry, novels, *immortality*. Alan's true gift to me, beyond the lush enjoyment of college friendship, would come later and be huge. He persuaded me to become a political being.

I was fortunate to spend remarkable summer vacations working outside of my own class. In 1961, one of my well-to-do New York aunts let me use her Sutton Square penthouse in order to write a novel. For six weeks, like a little pasha ensconced in a fringed litter atop a decorated elephant, I scribbled industriously in a pair of thick green notebooks. Then I took a break, got totally wasted at Malachy's on Madison Avenue, and met a crazy bald Greenwich Village musician who introduced me to a coked-up incoherent white blues singer, Fred Neil, who sent me for music lessons to a blind evangelical guitar player named the Reverend Gary Davis. This man and his wife occupied an improvised shanty house between project monoliths in a war zone of the Bronx.

I've always been impressionable. In my younger days I absorbed experiences with an exaggerated radioconductivity that left a powerful afterglow for *ages*. So it was when I discovered Damon Runyon . . . visited Taos and the Southwest . . . and met the Reverend Gary Davis. I hit the Bronx a handful of times, learning songs on guitar that I can still play with reasonable dexterity. The singer was a skilled musician, a disciplined teacher, a fascinating raconteur. He was terribly poor, a street preacher, full of pep, and still basically unknown. If I didn't get it right he *made* me get it right because how I played was his legacy. Even though his music was "religious," it was paramount to my transformation. I never feared a trip to his neighborhood, though it was shattered by poverty and governed by the rules of a harsh street. The romance of working-class vitality held me in its thrall.

When I received a draft notice midway through my senior year at Hamilton, my heart fell into my big toe. I had *no* desire to be in the army. That year I had been following Khrushchev and Kennedy's belligerent accusations of each other, and frankly their dramatic nuclear rhetoric made me nervous. Like: Who did those psychopathic tough guys think they were kidding? I was not pleased by Kennedy's enormous peacetime military budget and his army mobilizations. For a government class I'd written an essay on the U.S. presence in Southeast Asia, predicting that Uncle Sam would get bogged down in the anticommunist politics and muddy terrain of Laos. Though I think I had absorbed my country and my culture more than most, I had no more belief in patriotic rhetoric than I had in religion, 100 percent opportunity, or the Cubs chances to win a World Series.

A hockey injury had severed the anterior cruciate ligament in both my knees, so when I passed my first army physical, I screamed, demanding another chance to fail. In the next go-round I emphasized the injury, which an orthopedic doctor confirmed, and I was classified 4-F. Whew. Perhaps that scream was my first overt political act; yet for the moment it simply afforded me the opportunity to become a writer.

Graduating from Hamilton, I flew to Spain and lived with Mamita for a year. She gave me free room and board and the precious gift of time, during which I wrote another novel, my sixth, *The Sterile Cuckoo*. Mamita also taught me to speak Spanish and French—more transformative skills linking me to the wider universe. But to say that our social intercourse fell flat would be a vast understatement. Mamita pushed me to hobnob with her upper-crust friends, who bored and irritated me. When they started schmoozing about caviar and the caudillo (Franco), I wanted to karate chop them in their carotid arteries. Embarrassed that Mamita had a cook, a maid, and a chauffeur, I circumnavigated their attentions, causing dismay in the household. I made my own bed, shined my own shoes, and—horror of horrors!—fashioned my own sandwiches when hungry. Dinner with my grandmother mortified me because I couldn't stand to be waited on: shades of Peacock Point. Rarely would I travel in her car piloted by Felix the uniformed, horn-blowing chauffeur, because I *knew* the starving working people outside the windows hated our stinking guts.

Poor Mamita. At the end of the year I had a manuscript and two languages, paid for—by both of us—with ulcers. Mournfully, granny bid me adieu, and I, who should have been considerably more grateful, thanked my lucky stars and escaped to New York.

It was June 1963. With a manuscript in my heavy suitcase and only a few dollars gracing my pockets, I marched confidently off the boat to begin my after-life as F. Scott Fitznichols. What heavenly unfettered-ness! At last I was free! Though Manhattan was rife with relatives, I asked for nobody's help and quickly found myself a tiny apartment in a tenement on Prince and West Broadway for $42.50 a month. There was a sagging tin bed and a few rickety wooden school chairs; I built a desk and bookcases from junk scavenged on the streets. None of my relatives would visit, afraid to park their cars in a slum. That suited me fine; just let me be a bum and *write*. It wasn't that I could not afford a phone; I didn't *want* one. God, how I savored my liberty.

My spending habits were as frugal as always. I had no desire for material things (which I later real-ized is the first and most crucial commitment for an environmental—and any other kind of—activist). Most important to me then, accepting poverty gave me the absolute freedom to write. I am sure that my lust for a life in literature was a key factor urging me to cast my lot with the underdogs. Certainly it put me firmly on the side of "natural" environment.

For a while I lived without sheets or a telephone or almost any income at all. Chump change came in from an odd job dishwashing, or as a short-order cook, or playing my guitar in folk cafés on Bleecker and MacDougal Streets. But mostly I was fanatically producing books like some sort of extramanic Willy Wonka in a crazed literary chocolate factory. During that time I wrote and rewrote *The Sterile Cuckoo, The Wizard of Loneliness,* and several other never-to-be-published novels. One dealt with the last week in the life of a Bowery derelict; another chronicled the fall of a decadent robber baron family on Long Island's north shore; a third told of a kid who killed his brother in a hunting accident. I was happy and hung out at a MacDougal Street empanada stand frequented by noisy Latin Americans, mostly from Argentina, who were as penniless as me but brimming over with chutzpah. We chattered away in Spanish, horrified by the Birmingham church bombing that killed four black girls, disturbed by Buddhists protesting Diem in Vietnam, excited by Martin Luther King's "I have a dream" speech, and blown away by the movies *L'Avventura, La Dolce Vita,* and *Zorba the Greek.* I learned to play "Blowin' in the Wind" on my guitar, and Phil Ochs and I did a few sets together in Village cafés—"Strange Fruit" was a part of my repertoire. Kennedy's assassination affected me only slightly because I didn't like him at all and because I was totally absorbed in my personal acts of creation.

My college friend, Alan Howard, wrote to me from Guatemala, where he had a Fulbright grant and had fallen in love with a woman, Diana Oughton, who was in love with somebody else. "I wanted to tell you more about the stuff I'm getting mixed up in here," Alan wrote on October 25, 1963, "most importantly in literacy. Do you realize what you do to a man by teaching him to read & write, especially someone whose habits of living have not changed noticeably in the last 1000 years? It can mean the collapse of his entire universe, in fact, if you really make him literate, that's what it *has* to mean. Then you start asking yourself what right do you have to go around playing God, disrupting lives & playing with private destinies like toy blocks. And when I figure that out I'll let you know."

Although I don't have a copy of my response to Alan's quandary in Guatemala, it's clear that I poked fun at his earnestness. Perhaps I believed that his attitudes could be dangerous to me, collapsing *my* entire universe. After all, I was living on a shoestring; my chance to succeed as a writer was one in a million; and I must have known that in America politics and art don't mix, not after the McCarthy period they didn't. If I became a leftist, my chances of getting published would probably drop to one in a *billion* (if I didn't wind up on the hotsquat at Sing Sing first). So, despite my sympathy for his politics, I mocked Alan's drive toward the left, and received this reply from him dated January 17, 1964:

> John,
> You big bucket of shit. . . . Why do you still harp on this sterility of politics bit and its dichotomy with art? Politics is not simply elections and dull speeches by duller people. It is the dynamics of the social system in which we live, & that covers a lot of territory. Don't you think Hemingway, Steinbeck, Penn Warren,

even Fitzgerald (*Gatsby*) were interested, intently interested, in the way men organized their society? I'm looking at my bookcase—James, Chekhov, Greek Drama, Dickens, G.B.S., S. Lewis, Orwell, Vidal, Dostoyevsky (who spent I forget how many years in prison for a "political crime")! And shall I mention Agee? I have a book here of his I will save for you to read if you haven't already, *Let Us Now Praise Famous Men*. In short, I can not believe it is possible to write good literature without an acute conscience—not consciousness—for the conditions of one's society.

I refused to buy the rap. I was fiercely determined to be a writer and *nothing* would derail this ambition, and to that end I *had* to remain "free." For a year and a half I even avoided women, unwilling to risk any invasion of my creative space. For amusement I read books and newspapers, played my guitar, and marched around Greenwich Village observing the street characters, but I spent almost no money. Carefully, I measured the food I ate and never patronized a restaurant or entered a bar. Material needs would *never* impede my drive to be an artist.

Self-contained, content to be alone, as isolated from family as Axel Heyst had been on his island in *Victory,* I scribbled fiendishly, imbued with remarkable energy and concentration. Every few weeks I dropped *The Sterile Cuckoo* off at the front desk of another midtown publisher, then trotted home cheerfully to await its rejection while I worked on five other books and a passel of short stories.

But all too soon a terrible miracle happened.

In February 1964, I sold *The Sterile Cuckoo,* pocketed a five hundred-dollar advance, and, to celebrate, hopped on a bus to visit my best friend in Guatemala.

And Guatemala turned out to be a demarcation . . . an end to innocence . . . my Moby Dick.

"Do you realize what you do to a man," Alan had written me only a few months earlier, "by teaching him to read & write, especially someone whose habits of living have not changed noticeably in the last 1000 years?"

I was about to find out.

At the Mexico/Guatemala border a few miles south of Comitan, I ducked under a rope and climbed onto an old yellow school bus carrying an armed guard in a country at war with two guerrilla factions and just emerging from a state of siege. The dearth of wealth in Guatemala and the absolute lack of social compassion left me agog. It wasn't picturesque or romantic or soulful, and it was exponentially worse than anything I'd ever seen in Spain or the United States. For a moment I was thrilled by my Yankee power, lost my virginity to a prostitute, and had a fine old time. But the terrible poverty soon flooded my senses and perceptions with scenes impossible to ignore. Raw and nasty images still batter me from that brief visit. Young men deliberately maimed themselves to beg; kids went blind from filarial worms in their eyeballs. Whenever we got up from our fried chicken dinners at a sidewalk café sponsored by Purina, starving urchins vaulted the railing and scrambled to grab our bones before waiters shooed them away.

To elaborate on four scenes:

1. In front of the cathedral, Alan and I had arranged with a perky little man to purchase six marijuana cigarettes the next day. Come the appointed hour, I waited for him at the entrance to Alan's apartment building. The courier appeared but walked right past me in to the elevator. I followed, but he ignored me. The lift arrived, two people got out, we entered together, the doors closed, he punched the top floor button, and we started to rise. Nervously, I gave him the money and received four joints. "But you promised us six," I said. He begged me to let him keep two for himself. "But I gave you the *money*," I said angrily. "I *need* them," he pleaded. "I've got a habit but the boss never gives me any." "Dammit," I said, "give me those cigarettes, I *paid* you." Fumbling, he handed me another as the elevator continued rising. "One more," I snapped. "That's the deal!" He actually started crying, went down on his knees, gripped my pantlegs, and begged me to let him keep the final doobie. Confused and outraged, I was demanding that last cigarette when the elevator reached the top floor and the doors opened. Terrified, I leaped out, and the doors closed on the weeping courier, still on his knees, triumphantly brandishing the final cigarette.

2. I walked along a red-light street, eager to get laid again. Women, three to a crib, waited behind half-open Dutch doors. Stopping, I bartered with a young whore; her price was fifty cents. We went in back and she lay down on a cot. I removed all my clothes, hanging them on a peg; the girl had simply hiked up her dress. I was startled by the lack of artifice. On top of her, embarrassed, unable to get an erection, I pleaded for help, then gave up, apologized, and tried to kiss her: she turned her head away. Quickly, I dressed and fled, but stepped in her douche bucket like one of the Three Stooges on the way out, tipping it over and soaking my right foot. On the sidewalk, confused and ashamed, I must have realized that my lust for prostitutes was over. I would not yet have attributed this to "political" reasons or to a twinge of feminist sympathy, but that day was not far off.

3. For hours I sat on the roof of Alan's apartment building reading Émile Zola's novel, *Germinal*. Don't ask me why that novel, and why then—I have no recollection. Who recommended it to me? Had I brought it all the way from New York? Did it materialize out of thin Marxist air? Perhaps I filched it from Alan's bookcase. For those who don't know, *Germinal* tells of a French coal miner revolt. It is a panoramic saga of exploitation and revolution that fit Guatemala's turbulent mood. Across the street from Alan's place, three government judges waiting for a bus were gunned down by guerrillas speeding past. In a cantina I started a fight with a real live

World War II Aryan German *Nazi*! Newspaper head-lines daily announced the discovery of more bodies—tortured, beheaded, mutilated. Some Guatemalans that I spoke to admitted hating North Americans. Their country was a miserable satrapy controlled by the United Fruit Company. Everybody had a negative opinion about a CIA-scripted coup ten years earlier that had overthrown an elected government and commenced the dictatorial repression.

4. My buddy Alan's friend, Diana Oughton, was a Bryn Mawr graduate from a wealthy Illinois family. She worked for the American Friends in Chichicastenango. We visited her there. She was compassionate, and she despaired for the poor of Guatemala. Her family had come for a visit and loaned her their big American rental car. I fell in love with Diana's glamorous sister Carol, who got off the plane in a bright pink suit and paid me no attention. Diana drove us on a tour of the area, stopping once to pick up Quiche Indian hitch-hikers who obsequiously tried to pay her. Diana re-jected their money, almost breaking down in tears over the subservience and wage slavery of Guatemala. She was more ashamed of her parents' privilege than I had been of Mamita's. Back in the states, Diana sub-sequently joined the Weather Underground, began building bombs to protest Vietnam, and died in March 1970 in an accidental explosion on East Eleventh Street in New York.

One other note: In Guatemala I also met a guy my age named Michael Kimmel, who was destined to become one of my closest pals. A friend to both Alan and Diana, he worked for the Quakers, spoke Spanish fluently, could be even noisier and more annoying than me, and was highly politicized. Like Alan and me, Mike was determined to become a writer, and after he left Guatemala he began work on a novel called *The Master Weaver*, a loving and despairing portrait of the Maya Quiche people that would educate me further about that land.

Recently (1999) I researched the life of Che Guevara in order to write a screenplay about him. Che was in Guatemala City during the 1954 coup and it turned him into a revolutionary.

For me, ten years later, Guatemala was the Eden apple, the Pandora's box, the world knocking at my door. It magnified by a factor of one hundred the type of discomfort I had felt with Peacock Point, with segregation, with Mamita's Spanish servants. The real shock of the country was the degree to which its suffering could be considered an American creation, in large part due to United Fruit and other Yankee corporations that controlled the resources, the oligarchy, and the military suppression of the people. That made *me* to blame because I considered myself a true-blue American; hey, hadn't my direct ancestor signed the Declaration of Independence?

Don't get me wrong. I had fun in Guatemala (until dysentery laid me low). Yet I would soon use Guatemala as a springboard to inform myself of the cruel American history in the Caribbean and Central

America where we had helped lay waste to genera-tions of Latins by ruling them through petty tyrants schooled in North American counterinsurgency academies while we demolished their natural re-sources with a ruthless nineteenth-century planta-tion mentality. This was one way my country had become "the richest nation on earth." But now I had gotten an upsetting firsthand look at our wealth's origins—its human face—in Guatemala. Seventeen years had gone by between the punch I received for being a Dodger fan and the blow, now delivered by Guatemala, that similarly jolted me. I was twenty-three.

The haymaker did not catapult me into the Weather Underground, God forbid. Yet I left the country honestly disturbed by all the suffering that lay behind my well-being and unable to mock Alan's politics anymore. Bertolt Brecht certainly put his fin-ger on it when he wrote:

> They tell me: eat and drink. Be glad you have it!
> But how can I eat and drink
> When my food is snatched from the hungry
> And my glass of water belongs to the thirsty?

Guatemala could have pushed me into a radical politic, but it didn't. My writing career—my priority in life—hadn't even begun; *The Sterile Cuckoo* was yet to be published. Still, during the summer of 1964 Guatemala was the glass through which I viewed the signing of the Civil Rights Act and the deaths, in Mississippi, of the civil rights workers James Chaney, Andrew Goodman, and Michael Schwerner. Guatemala certainly helped open my eyes to the expanding conflict in Vietnam. Come autumn, I volunteered briefly in the presidential campaign of Lyndon Johnson, convinced (like everyone else I knew) that he was the peace candidate, and that Barry Goldwater, the bigoted reactionary from Arizona, would escalate the war and perhaps even use nuclear weapons on Asian people. Johnson was already maneuvering (after manufacturing the Tonkin Gulf Resolution) to realize Goldwater's vision. But I figured LBJ would never condone a situation in Southeast Asia like the one that oppressed Guatemala. His runaway election victory left me elated. By that time I had also come out of self-imposed hibernation to fall in love with my future wife, Ruth Harding—"Ruby."

When our new president immediately escalated the Asian war, I felt for the first time a personal sense of betrayal and outrage because of a politician's actions. Then LBJ sent twenty thousand Marines into the Dominican Republic, an act that coincided with our wedding. The August 1965 riots that shattered Watts in Los Angeles seemed like proper payback for the Vietnam escalation and the Dominican invasion. No longer disengaged now that I had sold a book and could begin to consider myself a writer, I was becoming a literate man ready for the collapse of his entire universe. Yet even as I now progressed toward that goal, I also fought it every step of the way. Why? Because my country had offered me the rewards and the "security" that seduces most of us to buy into the material holocaust. Even more importantly, my country was offering me the career of a professional American *writer*.

Trapped. Between capitalism and democracy!

After I returned to New York from Guatemala, the outer world hit my domain just as thugs had invaded Axel Heyst's island in *Victory*. My second novel, *The Wizard of Loneliness*, was sold and being prepared for publication. Lyndon Johnson was elected. I met Ruby. We got married and moved to a slightly larger apartment and installed a telephone. *The Sterile Cuckoo* went out on film option, and I was hired to write a screenplay. The book became a Literary Guild alternate. Avon paperbacks paid $37,500 for reprint rights, half of it mine. I was on a roll, but then Ruby's mother and father died within a year of each other. The new agent switched me from David McKay to G. P. Putnam's, where *Wizard* was being considered for a quarter million dollar prize that turned out to be a sham; writers were lured to sign with Putnam's, but nobody won the prize. The Vietnam War escalated. In California, working on *Sterile Cuckoo* with director Alan Pakula, I met Robert Redford, Natalie Wood, Roddy McDowell. Almost immediately it was difficult being married; at twenty-five I had no idea how to nurture a real relationship. My new lawyer argued with the agent and charged exorbitantly for doing my taxes. The Japanese bought translation rights for the *Cuckoo*. I bailed family members out of tax troubles, helped pay my younger brother's college tuition, and attempted to mediate dysfunctional family politics between my divorced parents.

Help!

This sudden deluge of money, obligation, and responsibility was seductive and also left me feeling as frantic and bewildered as that cartoon character, Wile E. Coyote, out beyond the edge of a cliff, spinning his legs in thin air just before dropping hundreds of feet to the nasty rocks below. How was I supposed to enjoy fame and fortune in such a whirlwind of gratuitous confusion?

It had taken me about five minutes to become terrified of the money.

Could I blame this on Guatemala? On who else, pray tell? Hindsight suggests that Guatemala became, in my imagination (as well as in my heart), a metaphor to explain the uncertain world that had suddenly pounced on me, lacking safety nets and other security devices, driven by rapacious economic forces, offering to make me famous if I would simply look the other way while everyone boffed the hookers. My literary success was accompanied by a sudden and cynical destabilization that quickly shattered any preconceived idealistic notions I might have held about the lofty Literary Life. It was 100 percent opportunity out there, with scant honor among the bandit negotiators. Every day I was pushed to make choices that were going to be riddled with either compromise or failure. In the back of my head I kept seeing those starving urchins scrambling for Purina chicken bones. Everything that now happened to me seemed to holler, "Watch out, Nichols, each step you take can lead to the moral abyss!" Maybe I exaggerate here, but it was soon impossible for me to think of writing, publishing, money, or marriage without weighing the consequences against Guatemala.

That miserable country was like a ghostly homeless person that I had to step over every time I started off in another direction with cash jingling in my pockets. Guatemala made it impossible for me to feel comfortable or free. Like it or not, Guatemala insisted that everything is interconnected and that the price of wealth for some is an ache of want for many. Ignoring this principle, we can run roughshod with impunity. Acknowledging it requires a whole new set of assumptions. It's not easy to be genuinely compassionate in America. You have to reject a *lot* of stuff that our economists hold to be self-evident.

When Alan Howard returned to New York in 1965 he took over my West Broadway apartment. Alan still loved Diana, a woman seriously radicalized by Central America. Ruby and I lived two blocks west in a six-floor walk-up on Sullivan Street with our fearless cat, Swoboda. When our son Luke was born in 1966, we found another small place on East Seventh Street. While my personal and professional world became cluttered and stressful, Alan and I spent much time together talking, drinking wine, shooting pool at Milady's Bar on Prince Street. Mike Kimmel visited often from Philadelphia, yammering about Cuba, Africa, the CPUSA. Guatemala had certainly changed my friends' perspectives. All three of us were writing novels, but Alan was sometimes exasperated with me because I still lacked a serious political commitment. Kimmel concurred, shitting on my inbred Floydian blue-blood upbringing, claiming, "There's no tragedy in dying races." Soon enough, Alan began to insist that I develop more of a social conscience. Eventually, this became a condition of our friendship.

I balked, frightened (and pissed off). Marriage and a new career were enough to handle. Please, let me enjoy my success: I had earned thirty-five thousand dollars in 1965, a preposterous sum (though now I was paying war taxes). *The Sterile Cuckoo* was on film option, and I had scored big-time on the paperback rights (then Avon published the book with a pornographic cover). My head shot, advertising *Cuckoo,* had appeared often in the *New York Times.* At literary parties I had chatted with George Plimpton, Iris Murdoch, Ralph Ellison. If I won the Putnam Prize I'd be super rich. Too, I was writing my ass off on other novels, I was on the brink of permanent success. How could a man in my position act against his own self-interest? Who wants to feel bad because *others* are suffering?

Give me a break, please.

If I bought into Alan's leftist political arguments, how could I enjoy my triumphs? Back at Hamilton, all of us burgeoning writers, artists, and musicians had dreamed about this type of glory. And believe me, when you've got the million-to-one shot in the palm of your hand, you just want to squeeze and hang on tight and to hell with Guatemala.

Alan gave me Charles and Mary Beard's two-volume work, *The Rise of American Civilization.* Grimly I read it, underlining the important stuff. Here was an American history not quite as cuddly as that of the Nichols and Floyds out on Long Island. Apparently, nothing about Manifest Destiny or the Monroe Doctrine jibed with the principles of our 1776 independence declaration. In light of our conquering past, the accelerating brutality of Vietnam made more sense to me. It was not the inadvertant aberration of an otherwise benevolent foreign policy, it was part of a historical momentum preordained . . . like my desire to screw prostitutes in Guatemala.

Hey, there was a *slave pen* in the Mastic attic!

The more I read, and the more I talked with Mike and Alan, and the more I thought about the war, the more I felt guilty about my own good fortune, . . . and I also began to question the validity of my "bourgeois" writing.

For a person of my limited intellectual and political sophistication, this was a downright foolish move.

Being married also changed everything on multiple levels. We live in a patriarchal society. There wasn't a blues tune I could sing where women were not sex objects, and most of the writers who shaped my literary sensibilities were men. My prep school and college were all-male institutions. And except for a few female tennis and track stars, my sports heroes were guys. On the whole, in our society women were as unequal as blacks or homosexuals, and in marriage, as well as in education or on the job, they were treated accordingly: as cheap labor, second-class citizens.

But Ruby and I got hitched on the cusp of radical challenges to the established order. Traditional structures defining our marital relationship were crumbling, and with difficulty we groped into a brave new world of flux, seeking not to impose limitations on each other. We argued about politics, about our commitment against the war, but had inadequate language for communication. We disagreed on how to handle the baby. New marital structures based on equality were contentious and threatening. Wanting to be open minded and progressive, I found myself daunted by my own emotional immaturity and sexist foundations that good intentions could not alter entirely. Despite a life of cultivating sympathy for underdogs, I had in me oodles of middle-class programming that made it difficult to go along.

Plus, I mean, hey, Jesus—why was everything suddenly so *serious*?

At night, as the sixties progressed, I lay in bed chewing my fingernails because I did—but did *not*—want to go there, giving up the stability that my dad had grieved the loss of long ago and that I knew was an illusion. Given the privilege (and the miracle) of my new writing career, it was horrible to admit—just when it seemed I had security within my grasp—that life would never be comfortable again.

I fantasized about running away to Las Vegas and shacking up in Caesar's Palace for the next five years with a trio of oversexed Jayne Mansfield look-alikes.

Instead, I finally cast a forlorn glance at the economic goodies and literary notoriety being offered me, then reluctantly turned my back on them. Yes, I took a walk. It was the "right thing" to do, but I hated it. So long to my literary success story. I knew I might never sell another book because I had no idea how to maintain my "integrity" on the commercial publishing fast track. I'd had it made but royally blew it. From 1965 on, however, all roads that I traveled went through Guatemala and Vietnam and marriage and parenthood. Vietnam, especially, became the quagmire that symbolized the need to question everything else. Opposition to the debacle soon absorbed my attention and included the study of history, culture, economics, sociology, environment, politics—you name it: the macroscopic overview. And as I questioned my country I also questioned myself. Since I remained desperate to salvage my new career, I decided to save it by developing a political art. I didn't realize at the time, but that decision is what eventually made me a *writer*. In 1965, though, it felt more as if I was going back to square one, and that step backward was absolutely no fun at all. How did a person live in just the "democracy" part of America?

Otto René Castillo, a Guatemalan poet, was exiled during the 1954 coup that politicized Che (while my Dad worked for the CIA and I witnessed the reaction to *Brown v. Board* at all-white Herndon High School). Castillo returned often to his homeland, eventually joining Luis Turcios Lima's left-wing guerrilla group, the Fuerzas Armadas Rebeldes (F.A.R.) in 1966. Castillo was captured by government forces in March 1967, tortured, and burned to death. Whenever I am asked to explain the road I've traveled, I read a poem he published in 1965. The poem states that one day the apolitical intellectuals of Guatemala will be interrogated by "the simplest / of our people," who will not ask them about Greek mythology or higher learning, but rather "what they did / when their nation died out / slowly, / like a sweet fire, / small and alone." The poem concludes:

> "What did you do when the poor
> suffered, when tenderness
> and life
> burned out in them?"

> Apolitical intellectuals
> of my sweet country,
> you will not be able to answer.

> A vulture of silence
> will eat your gut.
> Your own misery

will pick at your soul.
And you will be mute

in your shame.

It was simple: I did not want to be an apolitical intellectual.

Since I was a neophyte way out of his depth, however, politics now sabotaged my career. Trying to be responsible and polemical in my literature, I did rhetorical pratfalls instead, lacking (big-time!) the sophistication to meld bourgeois form and anti-imperialist content. Remember, I was sixty-ninth in a class of seventy-two at Loomis; we're not talking Einstein here. For help I pondered essays and exhortations by Noam Chomsky, I. F. Stone, William Appleman Williams, and Senator Fulbright. Seeking further guidelines, I reread Steinbeck, Upton Sinclair. At study groups I listened intently to theoretical discussions, eager to develop a more radical outlook and the skill to put it in books. I read *The Autobiography of Malcolm X, Down These Mean Streets,* by Piri Thomas, *Our Depleted Society,* by Seymour Melman, and wrote some propaganda flyers for SANE. I read Ida Tarbell's history of Standard Oil and Matthew Josephson on *The Politicos* and *The Robber Barons.* Rachel Carson's *Silent Spring* gave me serious pause. Bear in mind that to me a history of the Rockefellers or an analysis of Pentagon capitalism were as much an exposé of environmental problems as were Barry Commoner's *Closing Circle* or the Ehrlichs on the population bomb.

Any book on Vietnam I devoured immediately: *The Village of Ben Suc* (1969), by Jonathan Schell, would eventually hit hardest. The horrific environmental destruction advanced as our official policy of war seemed insanely apocalyptic—as indeed it was. It symbolized the United States' complete disregard for biological and human capital in its drive toward economic primacy going back to the eradication of the buffalo and the massacre of our Native peoples. Bombing, bulldozing, and defoliating Vietnam was a corporate endeavor akin to strip-mining Kentucky, creating Love Canal, or the Three Mile Island disaster. We did to Vietnam what Daniel Ludwig did to the Amazon and what Saddam Hussein would do twenty years later to Kuwait when he torched the oil wells. It was all shades of the Suffolk County Mosquito Commission's DDT spraying in the late 1940s at Mastic . . . times ten *thousand.*

America the Beautiful's dismaying Heart of Darkness.

I don't remember exactly when Mike Kimmel produced his initial draft of *The Master Weaver.* When I read it, Guatemala came painfully to life again. "Guatemala," the first paragraph began. "It's a republic, which is a simple thing, and, in its way, it's a nation. Guatemala, 'land of eternal spring,' sound of Guadalcanal, of Guantanamo, like a name you tend to forget because you don't speak the language. Guate-ma-la: soft syllables, sort of poetic, they mean Land of Many Trees."

Then I read Alan Howard's early drafts of a novel, which provided more details of that nation. Alan had already published two long articles in the *New York Times Magazine*. His first concerned the feeble literacy campaign in Guatemala, where 72 percent of the adults were unable to read or write in "the most illiterate country in Spanish America." Later, Alan returned south and contacted Turcios Lima's F.A.R. guerillas. Alan wrote a 1966 piece for the *Times Magazine* about the armed revolt in Guatemala, where 70 percent of the people worked land that "yielded just enough for survival," in a state with "one of the highest mortality rates in the world," where "a man's principal link to the national economy is as a cheap source of labor for the few hundred families that own most of the land."

My own first public attempts at political essays were written for my alma mater's newspaper, the *Hamilton Spectator,* which published seven of my efforts during the spring of 1966. One concerned a bloodless bullfight in the Houston Astrodome that caused a top Spanish torero to shame himself for an obscene amount of money. Another described the shock—and poverty—of Guatemala. A third mocked the absurd waste of funds in filmmaking. A fourth described the violent horrors of war in general. Then I gave them a nearly incoherent rant against our Vietnam policies. I was shrill and melodramatic—out of control. The writing was impelled by anger roused from my personal disillusionments and guilt, as well as from an objective analysis of unjust economic orders. Certainly my anger was in part selfish: I resented the obligations (and sacrifices) called for by a commitment, and I was terrified that I would not be able to succeed as a radical leftist writer. I also wanted so much to be an *American* writer like Hemingway, Carson McCullers, or Thomas Wolfe, and I could see that my dream was collapsing.

When my love of country turned to hate, I couldn't help but also hate myself.

Talk about downward spirals!

In late 1966 I sent a letter to the novelist Bernard Malamud, whom I much admired. I wrote care of his publisher and was amazed to receive a reply from Malamud himself before the week was out. My letter noted that in his most recent book, *The Fixer,* Malamud had stated there is "no such thing as an unpolitical man." Then I called attention to the professor, Levin, a character from his novel *A New Life,* who at one point worries that although he may be teaching students how to write, he isn't teaching them *what* to say and thus abdicates his social responsibilities. I confessed to being torn between art and activism and asked Malamud if he felt that writing was a valid act against atrocities like Vietnam. I ended with a final anguished cry: "I am worried I have not even started doing my part in keeping mankind from destroying itself!"

Malamud graciously replied that each writer had to work these things out for himself. He insisted, "In art, no compromise with the ideals of art." Then he suggested it was possible to write, teach, and engage in politics simultaneously. Toward the end he explained, "What a writer must say changes as he rids himself of provincialism, fear; yet he must always struggle to make it art."

Gratefully, I took his letter for permission to keep on writing books.

Shortly before Christmas 1966, I began to fashion an antiwar essay as a holiday gift for my brothers, Dave and Tim, who were seven and nine years younger than me and at risk in the draft. Dave would eventually file for conscientious objector; Tim eluded the army on medical grounds. In my cheery Noel essay I tied our Southeast Asia behavior to flaws of national character and history. For over a hundred pages, diatribe mixed with logical disquisition; passion and outrage described the fretful lunacy of war. The essay included a history of U.S. imperialism, some philosophizing about our national dissolution, and numerous references to the vapid ("fascist!") icons of American culture. Begging my brothers not to join the army, I had it in mind to save their lives.

Was it art? *Please.* But I had seriously embarked on a campaign to prove that content was more important than form. And this crusade kept me from writing another publishable novel for eight years.

The amazing thing is that it *didn't* render me

gaga, knitting formless purple sweaters on the ninth-floor lunatic ward at Bellevue Hospital.

Watching the war on television every day, I absorbed the human face of the suffering we caused and I wrote about it in my diary. Opening that record now, I find a page where I described the journalist Bernard Fall's last tape:

"My god," Fall cried, "they're shooting at a buffalo boy, they're shooting at buffaloes now, at this distance you can't even see what you're firing at!" American troops with Kodak Instamatics took pictures of rotting Viet Cong bodies. Sloppy southern voices ordered "motherfucking gooks" out of shacks while they put a torch to the village. GIs prodded women with kids at their breasts and hair blown into their eyes from chopper rotors. A peasant begged not to be taken, explaining that her children were sick and would die. A student admitted his father had been killed by Communists, but his town and country were being obliterated by Americans. He said, "My future is a tomb." When the time came to be drafted, he would choose the Communists. I quoted Fall talking about firepower in free-fire zones. "Firepower cannot be conceptualized intellectually, you just have to see it to know what it can do." There were gunships, rockets, bombs falling, explosions shuddering systematically through jungle trees, bubbles of flaming jelly and guavas. Followed by Americans praying to God and singing hymns, talking about Jesus. . . .

"It left me drained," I wrote in my diary, "almost on the verge of tears, just wanting to go out, buy a gun, shoot up something American, maybe a Hojo's, maybe the first soldier one sees in Times Square. Is there no pity—let alone reason, stability, creativity—in America?"

We killed four million Vietnamese over thirteen years in Indochina, and maimed millions more. Our bombing, bulldozing, land mining, and defoliation campaigns destroyed over 50 percent of the arable territory, leaving it toxic into the next century, an extraordinary environmental disaster at every level of human community structure and biological resources. Thanks to our war, the richest rice-exporting nation in Southeast Asia wound up importing almost all of its rice. Costs of the war led to huge budget deficits in America, environmental neglect at home, scaled-down social programs. I heard Martin Luther King at the United Nations declare that every bomb bursting in Vietnam exploded with a corresponding negative ferocity upon our own land and society.

As a person steeped in my American identity, I felt I was to blame, and during the war I lost my sense of humor, my perspective. I became scared, depressed, enraged. Ruby was uncertain about her own political commitment. Our marriage suffered accordingly. Our experience was common throughout the land.

When JFK was assassinated, Malcolm X declared that the "chickens had come home to roost." When the Vietnam War came to dominate my existence, it called forth all the discomforts I had felt over Peacock Point, DDT at Mastic, Harv on the grange hall steps, segregation pamphlets and Emmett Till, Chicano firefighters smoldering beneath the unfair demands of a racist straw boss, Josh White singing "Strange Fruit," the Pig Pool at Hamilton College, Mamita's servants, derelicts on New York's Bowery, and the kids chasing after Purina chicken bones in Guatemala. Add *The Grapes of Wrath* and *Silent Spring* and *Germinal*. Those were my chickens coming home to roost.

And I despaired.

The war transformed my life. You might say, Of course it did. Millions of Americans were affected. It transformed *all* our lives. But that's not true, is it? By and large, the war permanently changed only a small minority, but it never made for a kinder, gentler nation. We segued out of Richard Nixon into the Reagan–Bush era, then Bill Clinton. Now (today) that the balance of power maintained by the Cold War no longer limits worldwide capital expansion, the real agents of oppression have become NAFTA, the IMF and World Bank, and the World Trade Organization (WTO), which was vilified in December 1999 during the Battle of Seattle. We've decided that these organizations are a better way to skin the cat than brute military action, but the effects are similar. And when all else fails we still invade Panama, drop the bomb on Saddam, and level the Serbs' 'burbs. Racial divisions still define us, and why shouldn't they, given the economic barbarism we promote? George Jackson said, "Racism is a fundamental characteristic of monopoly capital." So is the plundering of natural resources leading to ozone holes, the greenhouse effect, the death of oceans and fresh water.

A few years ago I was contacted by the producers of a PBS documentary miniseries, *Making Sense of the Sixties*. They interviewed me on camera for two hours in a Santa Fe hotel room. How *had* the sixties affected me? Carefully, I described my political evolution and belief that through some form of socialist revolution we could reverse the environmental and social horrors of our time. In detail I explained how the sixties completely transformed my ideology, what I wrote, and how I wrote it. I listed the destructive traits of American capitalism and the injustices against people and natural resources that paid for them. I explained how Vietnam focused in me the daily human and ecological suffering that pays the bill for my comfortable life.

From my perspective, the completed miniseries was disappointing. Its sixties dealt with civil rights, Vietnam, and the counterculture through captivating and emotional images accompanied by a dearth of insightful class or political or economic analysis. Communism was mentioned often, but I don't think the word *capitalism* was uttered once. Many people outraged by the "democratic lie" seemed incapable of projecting alternatives. Not a second of my interview made the final cut, and no one else really addressed the kinds of radical ideas I had discussed. No doubt *Making Sense* was an accurate portrayal of how those days of rage were disappeared as if by Orwellian magic during the 1970s, when protesters rolled up their posters and returned to the system.

My name did appear, with thanks, in the credits.

Back in the sixties, wallowing in culture shock, career panic, a difficult marriage and child raising, my Movement participation was haphazard at best. I attended a gathering in Central Park where William Sloane Coffin spoke . . . and I joined a march down Fifth Avenue that was broken up at Forty-Second Street by cops on horseback who drove protesters backward through plate-glass windows. In October 1967, Ruby and I advanced on the Pentagon pushing year-old Luke in a stroller, and I actually made it up the steps to where lines of soldiers pointed rifles with fixed bayonets at us. I went to a few Movement for a Democratic Society meetings where Sol Yurick spoke, and I read all the literature from the 1968 occupation of Columbia University. But while Diana Oughton was being arrested repeatedly at demonstrations, I hesitated to adopt a line of action other than to write tracts and antiwar novels. Stubbornly, and desperately, I clung to being a writer. Unfortunately, the harder I worked at novels the worse they became and the guiltier I felt for not marching every day. But I was afraid that if I marched I would lose my toehold on a literary career and never be able to recapture it again. If I was going to be an activist I wanted to act through the medium that I *loved*. Was that courageous or cowardly?

Alan Howard gave me a copy of *The Wall,* John Hersey's moving tale about the Warsaw ghetto and its 1943 uprising. My journal states, "I think part of Al's reason for giving me the book is the way it treats peoples' commitment to resistance, the way they finally become involved." *Duh.* Alan then called my attention to Che Guevara's essay, "Man and Socialism in Cuba." After reading it, I wrote in my journal about the alienation of people from each other demanded by capitalist economic systems, and I conceded that a major aim of Che's socialism was to combat this alienation.

Che's essay also contained this sentence: "Let me say, at the risk of seeming ridiculous, that a true revolutionary is guided by great feelings of love."

I last saw Diana Oughton in 1969. She was seated on a ramshackle couch in my old (by now Alan's) West Broadway apartment. She had a cold, her cheeks were flushed, her voice was low and husky. On the wall behind her was a poster of Che Guevara with that quotation on it.

A year later Diana was dead. The house she died in stood next door to my great-aunt (author of *The Witch's Breed*) Susan Pulsifer's brownstone on West Eleventh Street. I can't presume to speak for Diana, nor can I say that I knew her except peripherally (through my best friend—Alan). But Diana's life and death had a major impact on me. She was deeply compassionate and had the courage of her convictions; she chose to act in a violent and revolutionary manner and paid with her life. There's no question in my mind that that is how great changes are brought about, as well as terrible repressions. We'd probably all like to think that democratic elections can reverse economic philosophies driving the engines of poverty and ecodestruction, but history—for example, Guatemala (1954), and Chile (1973)—suggests this is not possible. The United States backed Somoza in Nicaragua until the Sandinistas deposed him. We did not run Batista out of Cuba, Castro did. Haiti's Papa Doc Duvalier loved the America that approved his iron fist. Routinely, our electoral system has installed and maintained tyrannies. Violence was required to overthrow them.

It is tragic that political power often does come from the barrel of a gun. Certainly the United States does not negotiate on other terms, as Vietnam made clear, and the bombing of Serbia and Kosovo in 1999 reconfirmed. Corporations like Dupont and Halliburton succeed because they are supported by the largest military establishment on earth; their aggression against workers and natural resources is atomic in its savagery.

To some extent, those of us—and I am one—who protest peaceably and dream of nonviolent solutions have our heads in the sand. At best, we can spell things out, but ultimately the great changes are usually enforced by warriors.

Toward the end of the Cold War in the late

1980s, thirty-five nations were at war. As I write a decade later, seventy nations, or a third of the world's countries, are at war. The more that free-roaming capital dominates the global economy, the more guns will be raised, both in protest and to put down that protest. Throughout much of the Vietnam War, our government did not take nonviolent opposition at home seriously. But it was forced to take the VC seriously. That's why Diana was building bombs.

Yes, I chose books instead of bombs because I was *afraid.* I felt like an apolitical intellectual. Yet every day I also remembered that Bertolt Brecht had said a book was a weapon.

The darkest and most difficult year of my life was 1968. America's conduct of the war seemed like the transgression of a demented nation. As a taxpayer, a consumer, an artist, a father, a husband, and a citizen of the state, I felt responsible for its crimes. No dollar that I earned was innocent. And no aspect of resistance seemed to be effective.

I could not conceive how the war could continue, but it did. My constant outrage was exhausting. Everything I tried to write was so crippled by hostility and despair that it was ineffectual. The money from *Wizard* and *Sterile Cuckoo* dried up, and a third year passed without selling another novel.

Still, I wrote, fanatically determined to survive as a writer. I labored alone, alienated from the huge city around me and with nothing but failure to show for my work. I typed relentlessly on an autobiographical novel, *An American Child Supreme*. The book, a long-ago precursor to this essay, presumed to explain how a person like myself got from there to here, disillusioned by America's policies and values. It could have spoken for children of privilege, like Diana Oughton. My hero would get drunk at New York literary cocktail parties and uncork a litany for twenty pages against Vietnam atrocities. He was furious at his own loss of innocence. Like my father, he yearned for (and cursed) a stability of existence that did not exist. One version of the novel began with this paragraph:

> When I was a child I felt very safe because I really believed somebody had his finger on the Right Thing. Some adults, or brilliant persons, they were guiding it all in the Right Way, seeing that it went smoothly, and they were the guardians, too, of a really Moral Way of Living. So all you had to do was go along with this really Moral Way of Living and you'd always have your foot on a kind of base of absolute safety, and life would never be at all ambiguous or dangerous or contradictory.

The story's protagonist, Sammy Hauck, was drafted and killed in Vietnam. Or he fled civilization, disappearing into Alaska's wilderness. On another occasion he attacked a Manhattan cop and was shot dead. His bitterness came from the fact that his country—the youngest, richest, most energetic country on earth—based its miraculous prosperity on evil.

I struggled over many different drafts from 1966

until the mid-1970s. I wanted the book to be both a rhetorical and aesthetic masterpiece. But that was a pipe dream.

I explained my frustrations in a letter to my brother Dave:

> *An American Child Supreme* grew into a six hundred page monster. As I wrote along it seems I completely lost my cool, and my grip as an artist. Half polemic, half hysterical dogma, the writing went from sophistication in the early pages, to a crumbling ramble. It began as a fiction but kept running into and getting blown out of proportion by the truth. Real events merged with the fictionalized events, mucking up all balance. I was trying to write truthfully on false premises. Soul stuff got all mixed up with journalism; the whole thing became tense, jerky, wandery, completely unbalanced. . . . The basic problem was that I was changing myself as I was trying to write a novel about what myself was. Needless to say, I was operating without benefit of hindsight. But I was also overturning a lot of values I once held, not the least among them the purpose of art in general.

During this time, my friends Alan and Michael continued rewriting their stories about Guatemala. Mike's agent came close to placing *The Master Weaver* a couple of times, but in the end it was never published. Meanwhile, disgruntled by censorship and timidity at the *Times,* Alan veered to the left with his journalism when he became part of the Liberation News Service collective. For my part, *An American Child Supreme* went nowhere.

But I was like one of those unstoppable zombies from *Night of the Living Dead.*

Another book I started concerned a Native American professional baseball player drafted for Vietnam whose career was destroyed by friendly-fire shrapnel in his pitching arm. After he returned to his home reservation out west, government nerve gas testing destroyed his family's herd of sheep. To do research, I bused to Colorado Springs, rented a VW Beetle, and planned a trip through New Mexico and Arizona to gather facts about, and impressions of, Indian country. But Martin Luther King was assassinated the day I left New York, and my trip became a nightmare speed-demon journey where all I could do was drive, listen to the radio describe riots across America, and weep. In five days I covered two thousand miles, and got back on a bus for home. Not long after, Bobby Kennedy was killed, and then we had the Chicago police-riot Democratic convention.

I had a long discussion with my father that I described in my journal. I talked about our military spending and repression of Latin countries, also our "destruction of land, the waste, the packaging industries, 50 kinds of Cheez-Its, no-deposit no-return bottles, the incredible amount of energy spent, wasted in useless jobs, while real priorities like health, education, welfare don't get any bread—"

Pop had the audacity to suggest that one didn't

get far with violence and anarchy, and he made a further mistake by stating that the people in government were more sophisticated than the rebellious students.

"More 'sophisticated'?" I roared. What was so fucking sophisticated about "going in with B-52s and defoliants and soldiers and bulldozers and trying to solve the problem by just killing the shit out of everybody?"

That shut him up.

During the autumn of 1968 I wound up alone in the William Floyd house at Mastic, working on another novel called *Medal of Honor,* a bleak (what else?) story about a soldier who wins our highest military award, returns home, is feted by the president, then reenters civilian life only to discover it rife with racism, ignorance, environmental depredations, class warfare, you name it. By then I had the litany down pat. My hero, appalled by the true nature of the "democratic" monster in whose name he had butchered Asians, finally cracked, blew away his family and friends at a beachfront cocktail party, then staggered to the sandy shore and flung his medal of honor into the ocean.

Subtle I was not.

John Berger's *Art and Revolution* didn't appear until 1969, so chronologically it does not belong here; spiritually, however, it jibes just fine. "The present condition of the world, if accepted as it is," he wrote, "if approached with anything short of determined impatience to change it utterly, renders every value meaningless. Two-thirds of the people of the world are being robbed, exploited, deceived, constantly humiliated, condemned to the most abject and artificial poverty and denied as human beings." He declared, "The last need of imperialism is not for raw materials, exploited labour and controlled markets: it is for a mankind that counts for nothing." And that led him to conclude: "We have reached the stage of acquiring faculties—productive, scientific, cultural and spiritual faculties—which demand a world of equality. Either that demand is met or we deny our faculties and render our very being void."

I totally felt the void. My "art" was ineffectual and useless. New York City was crazy. I was ashamed of my American soul.

Nevertheless, part of my time at Mastic that September was wonderful. In the late afternoons I ran along sandy roads that wound through the forests. Rabbits sat on the paths and flickers flew away. Doves burst out of tree tops as I jogged by. I passed through fluffy storms of floating dandelion seeds and almost tripped over squirrels scurrying across my route. In my journal I wrote of a hawk swooping down into a rye field causing "hundreds of little birds to pop out from dry goldenrod stalks, almost bumping into me." The last monarch butterflies of summer fluttered dazedly out of my way. I felt as if I were jogging through the wonders of my childhood, that "natural" and naturalist world that had been gifted to me by my family long ago.

Weighed against the ongoing destruction of nature and human community in Southeast Asia, however, Mastic was now a heartbreakingly unreal (and vulnerable) place.

In my journal I wrote: *"Nothing we see in nature that is ours.* I think of so many friends who don't care about a beetle, or a plant; how many people I know are strangers to the land . . . would there ever be anything in them that would make them want to save it?"

My father was the last person born at the William Floyd estate, on September 17, 1916. His ashes entered the family graveyard a quarter mile from the house in May 1998. The house and those six hundred virgin acres—our family home since the early 1700s—had been the major reason Pop believed in a stability of existence that does not exist. He knew the desire for safety was hype, and he spent much of his life trying to live outside its clutches. By the time I spent my six-week swan song at Mastic in September and October 1968, I had evolved a far distance beyond the hype and was saying farewell to all that. By then our family had donated the Floyd estate to the National Park Service; when my grandmother died it would become a museum and wildlife refuge open to the public. That we chose to perpetuate roots, flora, and fauna instead of selling the place for a fortune speaks well of my family. Today, the William Floyd estate is a tiny piece of the Fire Island National Seashore.

While I sat miserably alone in 1968 at the old

kitchen table writing my antiwar novel and mourning the virulent human slaughter and ecodevastation across the seas, I also filled my journal with visions of the future that you would not think could be imagined in that quiet old colonial edifice surrounded by wild forests:

> He had terrible dreams of doom. Not of *1984* nor of *On The Beach*. Rather just of mess. Corruption, decay, pollution, apathy, things falling apart, general breakdown. The end of resources, total befouling of the environment, starvation, and the cruellest of all anarchies, the display at last of the core of man's soul. Shit in the streets and buildings crumbling of their own accord, avalanches of bricks like avalanches of melting snow, milewide jams of rancid Tampax floating in the molasses thick (and one day stopping its flow altogether) Hudson River, and air that suffocated people like an atmosphere of chocolate pudding, and a populace armed with outdated gasmasks that no longer worked, and every stalled broken down elevator in every urban skyscraper filled with putrid corpses. . . .

> That is where my journey had got me.
> We were "Destroying the world in order to save it."
> The apocalypse was now.
> *I had to get out of there.*

Eight months later, Ruby, Luke, and I moved to Taos, New Mexico. I don't remember exactly when the decision was made, but I knew that I had to flee New York, not to escape the need for commitment, but in order to find the will to make one that was viable. Ruby was more ambivalent about leaving the Apple. On our last night at the East Seventh Street apartment, we watched Neil Armstrong step on the moon. Naturally, I cursed the excessive costs of the space program while we waged war on Vietnam and our inner cities were collapsing. A few days later I celebrated my twenty-ninth birthday on the plains of Kansas. Unable to rent a place in Taos, we spent everything we had, eight thousand dollars, to buy a crude little adobe house on an acre and a half of land. Property ownership terrified me. I felt like I was William Randolph Hearst appropriating San Simeon!

That September I drove back to New York to pick up the last of our belongings. At the request of friends I drove uptown to Columbia one morning to help a group get out a fundraising letter on behalf of a peoples' clinica in Tierra Amarilla, New Mexico. At one point I flipped my car keys to a woman who needed to fetch more stamps and envelopes. Ten minutes later I received a phone call that my car had struck a five-year-old girl in Harlem. The child wound up on the critical list at a local hospital. The driver was a Black Panther and did not have a valid license. Witnesses claimed the little girl was at fault, popping out from between parked cars. But in New York a youngster that age could not be held legally responsible for an accident. The driver disappeared and left me holding the bag. I had to stand trial for loaning my car to an unlicensed person, a crime that could have cost me ten thousand dollars or a year in jail, or both. When I returned to New York for the trial, I was the only white man in a courtroom full of defendants, and the only defendant with a lawyer. Because of this, the judge called my case first and then threw it out because the officer who'd investigated the accident failed to appear. The victim survived, but for the next eight years I had a quarter of a million dollar lawsuit hanging over my head. Hence, two months after I had purchased my first property in life, my ownership of it was placed in serious jeopardy—the American Dream and its immediate flip side. By then, however, I was convinced that material things must not matter if you wish to remain sane in our culture. I had also decided that whether I earned five thousand dollars a year or one hundred thousand, I would always live a five-grand life in order to remain free and to minimize the damage I caused on earth. My attitude mitigated the effects of that car accident disaster. I no longer even remotely believed in a stability of existence that does not exist.

People often ask, Why did you move to Taos? I reply in a sane and pragmatic manner that New Mexico was almost the poorest state in America, closer to the Third World than to the First. A small number of the population controlled much of the wealth, meaning that class divisions were blatant and the resulting antagonisms could not possibly be ignored. For several years I had been reading about Reies Tijerina's land grant movement in the northern part of the state, and I was intrigued by those forthright politics of indigenous people demanding the return of their ancestral lands. Disillusioned by the system myself, I sympathized with native peoples allied against that system, a largely Spanish-speaking (and Indian) group descended from communal traditions antagonistic to more blatant private property and free enterprise shenanigans.

Because I was from a tricultural family myself, I needed to be in a multiethnic, multicultural area. I had only spent a week in Taos during the summer of 1957, but it had sure made an impression: Justin Locke's Spanish-speaking neighbors, the Pueblo, the intriguing town and its surrounding cultivated fields. No doubt I was drawn to Taos because of the blues and Woody Guthrie and the Reverend Gary Davis, because of Chicano and Mexican firefighters in the Chiricahua Mountains, because of my worker pals at the Maple Hill Restaurant in West Hartford and my Argentine friends at an empanada stand in Greenwich Village. Taos had ongoing history like my family had history, as well as a farm culture akin to the one I had been part of in Virginia. Most locals were "naturalists" too; they understood, and were caretakers of, their environment.

The imposing physical setting contained high mountains, sagebrush desert, the dramatic Rio Grande gorge. Yet forests around Taos were being heavily logged and sprayed with insecticides. Mine tailings had damaged the rivers. Pollution from power plants to the west was impacting air and water. And having watched for years as the United States systematically dismantled the Indochinese ecosystem, I yearned to make amends to land as well as to humanity.

But maybe the real reason I moved to Taos is that it was two thousand miles from New York.

During my first summer and autumn in Taos I paid attention to the soothing aspects of land. This enabled me to calm down and begin to operate more coherently. Yes, the mountains, mesas, and river gorge surrounding Taos were spectacular, wild, and original, but I related more to the prosaic terrain that shaped my immediate homestead.

Same as most of our neighbors, we planted a garden and had chickens, two goats (that I hated), and turkeys; I cut a half-acre hayfield by hand. Two irrigation ditches went through our small property, and we worked on them with nearby folks, a custom centuries old. We gathered wood in the forests and were taught to fish little mountain streams. Every night I put in my hours writing, trying (with brilliant lack of success) to fashion at last a political novel that *worked*. Fortunately, I also began to function at other levels that offered a bit of reward.

I went to meetings about the irrigation acequias, about the Taos Pueblo's battle to win back their Blue Lake land, about welfare cuts and a state adjudication suit of water rights, about nuclear waste disposal . . . and acid rain. Working with others, I became more attuned to the collective human experience on a scale I could comprehend. Soon I was writing for a muckraking journal called the *New Mexico Review* and playing hockey with its owner. Sometimes I helped get out mailings of a Chicano movement newspaper, *El Grito del Norte*. Ruby went on a Venceremos Brigade to Cuba and the FBI came up our driveway. There was a Moratorium Committee in town, and street demonstrations against police brutality, and a people's clinic that opened in the barrio of Santa Fe. I had research skills that were useful to local organizers. I began drawing political cartoons for an underground newspaper. And I joined an acequia organization opposing a government effort to impose a conservancy district and a large dam on the Taos Valley, a development sure to further destabilize a fragile ecosystem as well as village solidarity.

As Bernard Malamud had said in his 1966 letter, it *was* possible to write, teach, and engage in politics simultaneously. Out in the boondocks of northern New Mexico my provincialism began to wane.

At several gatherings a week I came in contact with a wide cross section of valley dwellers. These folks were friendly, humorous, and powerfully attached to their community. Although the Upper Ranchitos "village" where we lived lay only a mile from the Taos Plaza, it was a rural enclave. Our immediate neighbors accepted us into the fold with a relaxed generosity.

Tom Trujillo lived next door. He put his horse in

our front pasture and we worked on our fences together. Meliton Trujillo came across the Pueblo River
and sang corridos in my driveway. Eloy Pacheco, a
mayordomo (ditch boss), taught me to fix our acequia headgates. Adelecia Gallegos was treasurer of
the Mutual Domestic Water Users Association. The
plumber, Jerry Pacheco, labored like Hercules and
told a million jokes. Lucy Mares was a newspaper
columnist and a peppy organizer of the Senior
Olympics; her daughter, Stella, ran a beauty parlor.
Bernardo Trujillo was retired from the forest service,
a mayordomo on the Lovatos Ditch, and a guy who
loved to show me the ropes, *any* ropes. Isabel Vigil
and her daughter Evelyn ran an enchanted farm with
peacocks, pheasants, quail, ducks, geese, goats, burros,
horses, cattle, dogs, and cats up the yin-yang. Larry
Chávez was a mortician. John and Effie Sebastian
ran the corner cantina and convenience store. Gilbert
Medina earned a living as a molybdenum miner in
Questa, a half hour north of Taos; his wife Carmen
was a librarian.

Their welcome swallowed us up. Their laughter
made me laugh again. Their irreverence reminded me
of Damon Runyon. They were funny and very tough.
They argued with me and told tall tales; I attended a
handful of funerals. Every person had a history like
mine at Mastic, only centuries older and intertwined
with everyone else in the valley. Each inch of land in
the county bore their love and long-time roots.

What had never truly coalesced for me in New

York City now fell into place as I became active in grassroots endeavors. There was no great cathartic moment or a shout of "Eureka!" to hail a qualitative shift in my forward progress. But I lightened up and began to be useful on multiple levels as a researcher, an organizer, a member of two acequias, a newspaper reporter and editor, a general activist, and a neighbor involved with the daily life of our town. Never mind that I spent one more year, then two, then three fruitlessly belaboring bad novels. We had that acre of land to caretake with its two small hayfields, a miniscule orchard, barnyard fowl, a garden, and cottonwood trees. Having so much in common with our neighbors enabled us to thrive in a communal effort that was by definition environmental as well. "Back to earth" also meant back to people who were an integral part of the land, a fusion that's key to a social ecology. Community seals the deal.

For one of the more precious early blessings of Taos, I can also thank my friend Mike Kimmel. He came west and we hiked into the mountains, camping and fishing. We slept under the stars, shivered in hailstorms, marveled at the turbulent sierra weather. Hilarious misadventures gave both of us happy heart attacks. Regularly, over the next twenty-five years, Mike's intense love of wild country pushed me to enjoy that country with equal abandon.

Much that I had absorbed in New York now found application in New Mexico when I became a part of the whole. Our daughter, Tania, born in 1970, was

conceived because—even though almost destitute—
we could forsee a hopeful future. Citizens of the Taos
Valley, and the valley itself, were responsible for that
hopefulness.

It's, like, all of a sudden the sun came out.

One day a man named Alfredo Pacheco brought his
sow to Upper Ranchitos to be bred. My neighbor,
Steve Mondragon, had a boar who was tops in his
field. At some point during their fervid interaction,
Pacheco's sow broke free of the pen and lit out toward her destiny. A quarter mile to the south lay my
innocent adobe home and prosperous vegetable garden. On the portal sat yours truly and Mike Kimmel,
who was out west to hunt and fish. We each had
a glass of Jack Daniels in hand and were discussing
Keats and Baudelaire. Some annoying foreign sound,
perhaps a loud grunt, caused us both to glance up.
Pacheco's sow had already chewed down a row of
my broccoli and knocked over a fence of peas. "Hey!"
I hollered, bolting up as she snuffled among the
squash. Mike, a diminutive fellow, tried to head her
south; she charged and bowled him over while I
fashioned a clothesline lariat. That big pig was *scary*.
She grabbed a tomato plant and manhandled it like
a cat shaking a rat. I fitted a noose around her neck,
but she yanked me to hell and back, so I let go
pretty quick. Finally, our insults and a flurry of small
boulders sent her packing. A few minutes later
Alfredo Pacheco ambled up with a frown on his

sunburned face and a Hamm's beer can in his rear pocket.

Had we seen his sow?

One thing led to another, and soon we were in my kitchen playing guitars, singing ranchera songs, and downing boilermakers. Pacheco had read all of Hemingway and even a bit of Joyce. Kimmel was more interested in his voluminous fishing expertise. And I wanted to know more about the wife he had loved and then lost when she simply disappeared.

That's how novels are born.

I had sold a second book, *The Wizard of Loneliness,* in 1965. My third published novel, *The Milagro Beanfield War,* came out in 1974 and salvaged my life as a writer, breaking a nine-year drought initiated by that visit to Guatemala. It was at last a political payoff, a piece of quasi-effective propaganda. *Milagro* incorporated many of the unpublished books I had written going back to *The Journey* in 1957. It personified the struggle against racial prejudice of *Don't Be Forlorn* (1960). The novel never would have been written without the trip to Guatemala or Alan Howard's insistence upon social action. The story owes its compassion to Diana Oughton's despair over the terrible treatment of native people in Chichicastenango and to Mike Kimmel's *Master Weaver. Milagro* came directly out of the crucible of Vietnam and would have been impossible without my years of raging against the war. My struggle with Ruby to define a more liberated marriage is an important part of the novel, along with repercussions from her trip to Cuba. *An American Child Supreme* is there on every page; also *Medal of Honor;* and my story of a Native American baseball prodigy whose reservation's sheep herds were decimated by nerve gas. Mastic and my family's love of the land and our naturalist tradition are important to the book. So are Malcolm X, Ida Tarbell, Rachel Carson, *Germinal,* and John Berger's political line from *Art and Revolution.* The class struggle that disturbed and shaped me going back to Emerick Tedesky's anti-Dodgers haymaker and the servants at Peacock Point are everywhere evident in that novel . . . and in my work that has followed since. People often suggest that *Milagro* is an exclusive product of New Mexico, but that's not accurate: 90 percent of the book is universal. This area was the catalyst that gave me a language, theater, events, and *people* to express beliefs that had been hammered out by a lifetime's experience leading up to Taos. New Mexico then accepted, and nourished, my roots.

Over the next twenty-seven years, though I have been torn between what you might call a hands-on activism and writing books, my politics have not wavered. I understand now that novels and essays are valid stones on the barricades, but it took me a long time to reach—and to accept—this conclusion, and I've never honestly been comfortable with it. My career has been fitful, uneven, and my life chaotic and crudely disciplined. Many of the books I write still don't get published because they're about as bad as writing gets. I have speechified, organized, leafletted, fellow traveled, demonstrated, protested, gone on strike, done benefits, tried to write propaganda, hoped to produce a radical art. My concerns have been local, national, universal—all over the map. Since 1980 I have also written screenplays for movies that were mostly unproduced, although the Costa-Gavras film *Missing,* which I rewrote before shooting, made a valid political statement against U.S. policies in Latin America that I had witnessed firsthand in Guatemala. And the *Milagro* movie on which I shared a credit is a compassionate film, although it pales compared to one of its New Mexico forbears (and major inspirations), *Salt of the Earth.*

Why movies? Because on the whole Hollywood's product is reactionary, yet it wields enormous power around the globe. This behooves us to create antidote works of a more progressive nature. So projects that I wrote dealt with Haitian refugees, nuclear holocaust, science and human values in the twentieth century, Kayapo Indian rights in Amazonia, Pancho Villa and the Mexican Revolution, the life of Che Guevara. It's important for me to point out that while I live in a small New Mexico town, much of my work has been international in scope.

Other novels among my published works range from a treatise on the violence underlying our culture *(American Blood),* to the dysfunction of the marriage institution *(Conjugal Bliss),* to a satire of the self-absorbed me generation *(The Nirvana Blues).* The novel I care about most, *The Magic Journey* (1978), contains everything in my macroscopic overview that I feel defines life as well as seeks to destroy it. The book is a plea for social commitment and no more regional than the Bible. Yes, I am a humble, self-effacing egomaniac, but I'm also proud to say that except for *American Blood,* my other stuff is rich in laughter. You can't overthrow the jerks without an ironclad indestructible sense of humor.

Manuscripts I have never published, of which there are many, include one Sisyphean monster that I've belabored for twelve years (1988–2000). Titled *The Voice of the Butterfly,* it is a slapstick Keystone Kops satire of the impending social and environmental holocaust. It could be set anywhere. Uninformed readers may call my heroes monkey wrenchers; I'd rather define them as "liberation ecologists." Liberation ecology, the militant arm of social ecology, recognizes that all life is sacred and that nothing short of total revolution based on biocentric ideas *and* human equality can save the planet.

"In biocentric thinking," explains David Morris, "no single species has dominion over the earth. The earth instead is viewed as a community where human and nonhuman life are intricately entwined, where all species live and develop together, where the biosphere, not humanity, occupies the center." But I presume we will never be willing or able to think and act in this gracious way until all "men" are first created equal.

My half-dozen nonfiction books that record the rhythms of the Taos Valley are quieter than the fiction, less overtly political, easier to identify as "environmental." Some are full of my photographs, downright serene and pastoral. I could pass an eternity of twilights on the mesa contemplating sagebrush and sky. It bears repeating, however: I was raised to understand that *all* of the natural world is interconnected and that the human species is a part of the natural world. No majestic cloud formation is free of toxaphene or a farmer's need for rain. My father studied bird and animal behavior and human interactions on an equal and interchangeable plane. It was understood that DDT spraying and the Hiroshima bomb, as well as African drought and volcanic eruptions, were all natural disasters. Human perturbation of earth, air, and water is as natural as the last ice age was natural. Inner city socioeconomics are as natural as weather in Yellowstone. Human rights and environmental rights are the same and inseparable. The works of Aldo Leopold and John Muir, along with Karl Marx and Adam Smith, are equally about environment and should never be separated. If we all viewed humanity's actions as integral in this way, perhaps we'd have a better shot at modifying our behavior to the benefit of all environment. So far, our inability to understand this has been catastrophic.

We lack a biocentric perspective, and we have not even remotely evolved a social ecology.

(After writing that last sentence, I see myself as Lily Tomlin in pigtails, a jumper, and Mary Janes, seated in an oversize rocking chair with my tongue stuck out, saying, "*And that's the truth!*")

Time flies, and I'm already sixty years old. Diana Oughton died thirty years ago. After a full career as a progressive journalist and labor organizer, Alan Howard is still at the top of his game. Mike Kimmel dropped dead at fifty-seven in 1997. He never quit writing novels, though none were ever published. One of his last, *Banished,* was a cynical and bitter rant against the virtual genocide carried out by the Guatemalan government against its Indian population.

Myself, after three divorces, two grown kids, one grandchild, sixteen (published) books, and one open-heart surgery, I live alone in a diminutive place crammed with filing cabinets, books, tables, and desks overflowing with manuscripts, papers, magazines, and newspapers. It's not much different from the tiny apartment on West Broadway and Prince Street where I began my afterlife in 1963. Perhaps because I never cared for the money, there have been stages in my convoluted career where publishers and movie studios threw it at me in droves. *Go ahead, John, take it, live it up!* the Devil cackled. With characteristic discomfort I quickly doled out the loot and there's no evidence of its existence today. Pardon my run-on sanctimony, but why consume beyond my simple needs? I don't want my desires to make others hungry, level forests, or contribute to the greenhouse effect. As I've explained, my freedom to write always depended on living poor, and that attitude has served me well. If you don't buy into the system, the system should not be able to control you. Put another way by the socialist poet Walter Lowenfels:

"When the tragedy of the world market no longer dominates our existence, unexpected gradations of being in love with being here will emerge."

When I moved to Taos in 1969 I returned to being in love with being here. That went hand in hand with Che's "great feelings of love." You can't agitate for positive changes on earth from any other perspective.

So how would I conduct a summing up, state my credo, and then get out of here? Well, I'm no cynic, but over the last three decades I have watched, astonished, as both Taos and the planet strive to self-destruct, while the sort of revolutionary passions that rocked and changed me and many others during the 1960s have been co-opted and fuddled by forces tied to the global economy. The fall of the Berlin Wall in 1989 exacerbated the problem by removing all restraints to the free flow of capital everywhere. Today, many First World environmental and radical social organizations are unfocused and beset by specialization, infighting, lack of vision. If you ask me, deep ecology won't work, nor will communism, capitalism, or postmodern deconstructed utopian sustainability.

World Watch is cutting its own throat by trying to figure out a *polite* way to reproach the masters of industry. And the United Nations couldn't halt a bloodbath if it wanted to. Even as we map the human genome, we increasingly lack the will to visualize *the overall picture.* This suggests that the propaganda—the *brainwashing*—arm of globalization has stifled the human imagination. We are mesmerized by the idea of growth, science, the green revolution. When Chicken Little cries "Greenhouse effect!" "Ozone hole!" or "Rampant diabetes!" even the craziest eco-sociopaths among us are afraid to retort, "Revolution!" Instead we bark, "Earth first! Save the toad! ZPG!"

"Such is the word dodge," wrote Roque Dalton, a Salvadoran poet, many years ago. "To denounce the infinite generality of evil / while proposing solutions the size of an ant."

Myself, I do not have the courage or the fanaticism that motivated Diana Oughton to build bombs, but I cannot envision the changes we need without some sort of apocalyptic reaction against the current levels of violence generated by the daily economic activities of the multinationals that feed and clothe us. Territorial shooting wars are only a small fraction of the greater (and more horrific) violence of a world market that levels forests, pollutes the oceans, impoverishes people, and toxifies topsoil in order to bring us our hamburgers, polyester golf slacks, and Marlboro cigarettes. "The human murder by poverty in Latin America is secret," writes Eduardo Galeano.

"Every year, without making a sound, three Hiroshima bombs explode over communities that have become accustomed to suffering with clenched teeth. This systematic violence is not apparent but is real and constantly increasing: its holocausts are not made known in the sensational press but in Food and Agricultural Organization statistics."

Significant literature on this potentially terminal disruption is available yet widely ignored. In it our expanding biological wasteland is rarely tied coherently to class analysis, a flaw that tragically compromises the information. I believe there's no way to address a collapsing biosphere without first recognizing the core issue.

To whit:

Most work that keeps the world humming is the province of working-class or peasant-class human beings who comprise the planet's suffering underdogs. Environmental collapse is now universally caused by monopoly capital plundering earth's biological and human resources for profit. The profit is generated by the labor of those underdogs, whose energy is thus co-opted to destroy environment. This means that our most destructive environmental problems are tied to their inequality, which determines all wars and all so-called "natural" disasters. That inequality is causing a downward social spiral on earth and ecodevastation. Profit requires demolition. The racism that deforms our nation (and the globe) is a tool used by a capitalist society to maintain class divisions for profit-making reasons, so racism is also a main component of biosystem toxicity. The ozone holes, the greenhouse effect, the extinction of species are all a direct result of oppressing Guatemalans, starving Somalis, and jailing inner-city Philadelphians. Similar processes created both Chernobyl and Pinochet's dictatorship in Chile. You might as well call Bhopal, India, another Love Canal, New York, and think of death squads in Columbia as one of the advertising arms of General Motors or Coca-Cola. You cannot separate massive social injustice from the clear-cutting of a rain forest. The collapse of ocean fisheries is directly connected to the lack of education, housing, and health care in Haiti and Peru.

In his book *Divided Planet: The Ecology of Rich and Poor,* Tom Athanasiou puts it this way: "The urban-industrial, export-based models of modernization and social improvement . . . have caused human suffering and ecological destruction on a grand scale." He describes how development is based on every sort of crime against the natural and human world. He explains that if we are to survive, markets must learn to function without expansion and without wars. "A transition to an ecological society must involve a vast increase in justice and democracy; unfortunately, this does not seem to be the direction of history. . . . Capitalism is triumphant. It has its many variations, but few glorify equity or justice, and few are kind to 'the losers.'"

Speaking of environmentalists, Athanasiou says, "The time for such political innocence is over. This has been a dark century, but the planet is wavering at the edge of even darker possibilities. Given the key role they are fated to play in the politics of an ever-shrinking world, it is past time for environmentalists to face their own history, in which they have too often stood not for justice and freedom, or even for realism, but merely for the comforts and aesthetics of affluent nature lovers. They have no choice. History will judge greens by whether they stand with the world's poor."

When anyone speaks of the poor, I think of Guatemala. The first time I truly realized how poor poor can be was in 1964.

I have followed the progress of Guatemala since then because it is the catalyst that woke me up and shaped the politics of my two best friends. Guatemala has been our *personal* satrapy.

Over the last thirty-five years, while I was evolving into the rational and well-fed human being who cranked out this essay, Guatemala was going through hell. In that country the Vietnam War never ended. The human suffering there created by our lifestyle here is much worse now than when I visited long ago, yet, so far as I know, no First World college students ever occupied an administration building on behalf of the Quiche Maya. But because Guatemala is *the* enduring symbol of earth's downward social spiral and environmental collapse, I'm going to dwell on it again. History will judge greens by whether you listen to me or not.

In a nutshell, Guatemala is still the richest state

in Central America, providing us coffee, bananas, sugar, beef, and cotton. We are her biggest trading partner, purchasing 41 percent of exports, providing 39 percent of imports. Four hundred U.S. firms have investments in Guatemala, of which ninety are among the top five hundred corporations in the United States. Since 1954 we have provided substantial military and government aid to keep these investments stable. In the late sixties and throughout the seventies, we supported the army's civic action and counterinsurgency programs, which evolved into a policy of ethnocide against indigenous peoples. Jimmy Carter's administration withheld aid because of those human rights abuses; the Reagan administration returned to business as usual.

In a 1989 Guatemala country guide published by the Inter-Hemispheric Education Resource Center of Albuquerque, Tom Barry wrote: "Repression seems an almost natural part of the climate in Guatemala. So final is the repression that the country has no political prisoners—there are just bodies and disappearances."

Because of the CIA-administered coup in 1954 and our aid and support ever since, Guatemala is essentially a Yankee creation. Yet to most North Americans outside of the Pentagon and a few corporate headquarters, that country was invisible when I went there in 1964, and it remains invisible today. Why? Because Guatemala's misery is exponentially proportionate to our well-being, but we childishly ignore it to absolve ourselves from guilt.

No housewife in Peoria consciously wants to admit that her bananas are procured by U.S.-allied death squads, but that is a fact and has been so for a while. You can read all about it in the books of 1967 Guatemalan Nobel laureate Miguel Angel Asturias—most notably, *El Señor Presidente*. You can read all about it in the autobiography—*I, Rigoberta Menchú*—of a Guatemalan Quiche organizer awarded the Nobel Peace Prize in 1992. And you can read all about it in Noam Chomsky's 1993 introduction to Jennifer Harbury's *Bridge of Courage*, the collected testimonies of Guatemalan rebels.

Chomsky recalls a history of American-backed atrocity across Guatemala in the 1980s that reached "epic levels of barbarism as the U.S. campaign against democracy and social justice moved into high gear throughout the region. Over 440 villages were demolished, huge areas of the highlands were destroyed in a frenzy of possibly irreversible environmental devastation, and well over 100,000 civilians were killed or 'disappeared.' . . . All of this proceeded with the enthusiastic acclaim of the Reagan administration."

In his 1991 novel, *Banished*, my friend Mike Kimmel angrily described that ethnocide, which sent hundreds of thousands of Guatemalans into exile:

> They herded the people inside and the screams commenced and a head, Efrain Garcia's, was tossed out the window, and another, Caesar Lucas', and another, and the children cried and the adults groaned. Lydia kneeled by her

moaning mother. The twins bawled. Soldiers rushed here and there, plucking victims, dragging them into the classroom. Saturnino recognized Nacha's scream and wept. . . .

So they killed 50 more, twice, making it 120, roughly 70 percent of them male. Which wasn't demographically sound, but it certainly put the fear of God in the rest. Besides, not all that many of the female survivors were going to be fertile after this shock. The Indians screamed and wept and moaned and the soldiers busted heads and limbs and fired away with their M-16s until Sebastiani said stop.

"It is eleven-forty," he told the survivors. "You have been banished from this republic, I told you. Now you have until one o'clock to be on the road to hell or Mexico. By two o'clock this village will be history, embers. You will have absolutely no reason to be here."

Even without the systematic murders numbing a nation that the United States promised in 1954 would become a "showcase for Democracy," one wonders how any sane Guatemalan could feel "a reason to be there." According to Tom Barry:

> Fewer than 2 percent of the landowners own 65 percent of the farmland. . . . One result of this skewed land distribution is that 80 percent of rural Guatemalans live in absolute poverty, unable even to satisfy their most basic needs. . . .
>
> So severe and widespread are hunger, malnutrition, and illness in Guatemala that they

can only be described as a type of social violence. . . .

Guatemala wins the unenviable awards for the highest rates of infant mortality, illiteracy, and malnutrition in the region, while offering the lowest life expectancy, and the least amount spent on health care per person. . . .

[Guatemala] is . . . an environment devastated by distorted patterns of land use, a counterinsurgency war, and a search for survival by the peasant population. . . . An estimated 25 to 35 percent of the land cover is considered eroded or seriously degraded.

Excessive pesticide use renders farm labor . . . dangerous work. Along the littoral highway . . . billboards advertise chemicals which are banned in the United States. The chemical fog that clings to these flatlands leaves your eyes smarting and your lungs gasping for breath. . . . Guatemalans are said to have more DDT in their body fat than any other society.

Although that was written a decade ago, little has changed. Some late-breaking news is that the counterinsurgency war finally "ended" with a cease-fire. The violence and poverty continue, but last year a Guatemalan Human Rights Commission was allowed for the first time to detail decades of tragic abuse unleashed after the 1954 coup. Why has this abuse been both tacitly and actively promoted or at least condoned by the United States?

Because our wealth is based on it.

And that is the number one environmental problem on earth.

Three decades after Otto René Castillo published "Apolitical Intellectuals," Noam Chomsky asked:

"Who created 'the situation that gives rise to violence'? Who refused to listen to the screams of children being brutally murdered or dying from starvation and disease, because there are pleasanter things to do? Who paid taxes quietly and unthinkingly, helping to ensure that torture, massacre, and indescribable suffering continue, while doing nothing to end these crimes—or worse, justifying and abetting them? Who joined in the torrents of self-praise that pour forth in sickening abundance, keeping eyes carefully averted from what we have actually done with our huge resources and incomparable advantages? Who are the real barbarians?"

I.e.: Who cares about Guatemala?

Who among us stands with the poor?

I'm holding in my hand a Xerox of the front page of *Prensa Libre,* a Guatemala City newspaper, dated March 14, 1996. In a large photograph, Alan Howard is greeting Reynaldo González, general secretary of the Union of Banking and Insurance Employees of Guatemala. González's life had been threatened by death squads; Alan, as a representative of UNITE— the Union of Needletrades, Industrial, and Textile Employees—was in Guatemala to offer protection and get Reynaldo safely out of the country. For years

Alan has actively organized to obtain benefits for sweatshop workers in the Caribbean, Central America, and elsewhere.

"You know," Alan wrote to me in August 1995, "some of the union work I have been doing lately has brought me back to Latin America, basically helping to build unions there, which I find incredibly exciting because it re-connects me to that original impulse and experience in Guatemala which I know hit you in a similar way. It changed my life, made me a marked man. I tried to get this idea into that essay I wrote . . . the idea that the kind of massive poverty we saw in Guatemala, and of course soon learned could be found all too abundantly throughout the world, was an outrage, a disaster, a horror—"

Alan stands with the poor.

And I still care about the land that altered my life, forcing me to build a social conscience. A land that made me yearn to change the status quo, raising my voice against the oncoming nightmare. I could never forget that country because it *is* the oncoming nightmare. The contents of all my books since 1964 have been shaped to some extent by Guatemala. Today, Guatemala remains that ghostly homeless person that I have to step over every time I start off in another direction with cash jingling in my pockets.

The world at large is far more Guatemala than it is middle-class North Americans blythely bathing in hot tubs or crowing, "Oh what a feeling, Toyota!" Guatemala *is* the poor. It is the reality and the symbol, the metaphor, the past and the future, the *idea* that makes me write propaganda when I would rather play.

But I am a hopeful human being, and here's one reason why. Twenty years after the trip to Guatemala that nudged me into the maelstrom, I returned to Central America. This time, though I had far different reasons for visiting, I also received an elemental gift.

Shortly before Christmas 1983, I spent ten days in the former U.S. colony of Nicaragua, traveling and speaking with people as part of a tour organized by the Office of the Americas in Los Angeles. At that moment, the United States had stepped up sabotage efforts and was funding a Contra war against the ruling Sandinistas, who'd overthrown a dictatorship that had kept Nicaragua as bad off as Guatemala for decades in order to benefit *us*. Managua expected an American invasion soon, and, because of the Contras, entire towns had been evacuated from the northern border with Honduras. Everywhere, civil defense groups were digging bomb shelters, and it seemed the entire citizenry carried AK-47s.

Nicaragua was very poor and her citizens had long suffered major deprivations. Yet there was a spirit to the country that made it radically different from the Guatemala I had visited a generation earlier. People who'd won an insurrection in 1979 against the U.S.-supported Somoza dictatorship had hope and extraordinary good humor. They operated from a remarkable sense of historical purpose and took great pride in their revolution, believing that now they could share a wealth created by their own natural resources. Actual freedom *(democracy!)* was possible. They were organizing around literacy programs, health care, housing, jobs, education, unions, cultural awareness, conservation projects, feminism, human rights, liberation theology, economic equality. Imagine an entire country tuned into a macroscopic overview and imbued with the joy of being here.

Caught up in their fervor, I was transfixed and happy and intoxicated. Never in my own country had I experienced comparable idealism and togetherness.

One evening our group attended the National Circus. Three hundred people had assembled under a blue and yellow tent. At the start of the program a folkloric dance troupe bounded into the single small ring, and somebody outdoors beside the generators flipped a switch, turning on a blaze of floodlights. This immediately blew a fuse and plunged the tent into total darkness. The four-piece band and the dancers froze while technicians frantically searched for another fuse. Moments later, the lights blazed on again, the band struck a high note, the dancers began to leap and twirl, and then another fuse blew. Spectators cheered, and this time the orchestra and the intrepid dancers continued in the dark. At that moment, several onlookers with flashlights stood up and shined them at the dancers while the tiny band played on. The crowd burst into wild applause.

The woman beside me turned, a delighted

sparkle—and the hint of a tear—in her eyes: "For a little country with all its borders under attack," she murmured, "this is *incredible*."

It *was* incredible, and I brought a positive Nicaragua back with me to Taos just as I had brought a negative Guatemala back to New York a lifetime ago. In the early 1980s, many of our recent domestic gains in civil and human rights (and environmental protection) were under attack as part of a Republican plan that also aimed to reincarcerate liberated Nicaragua. Nicaragua itself was about to learn that no tiny "banana republic" can sever its chains if we decree otherwise.

But the precious gift that Nicaragua gave to me, and that I carried back to Taos, was a knowledge that revolution is actually *possible*. Revolutions can get made, even against a superpower; history is change personified, and the underdogs do have a chance. For any organizer this knowledge is a must.

And those ten days in Nicaragua remain a *compañero* that travels beside me, infusing everything I do with optimism, no matter what.

My conclusions? I surmise that for the world to continue with any physical integrity we must eliminate expanding GNPs, freeze or reduce human populations, create sustainable markets based on sound ecological principles instead of profit, redistribute a finite wealth evenly, halt the extinction of species, and get rid of much pollution. This effort will require the collaboration of all peoples in unison or it will fail. Barry Commoner said long ago, "The world will survive the environmental crisis as a whole, or not at all." Majority rule is required for success, and the poor are that majority.

So it's simple: To survive, *everyone* must stand with the poor.

But we are far from that reality now because we haves on the planet deliberately ignore the unfortunate majority of have-nots. *The human murder by poverty in Latin America is secret.* What do you suppose is the current ratio of capitalism to democracy in the United States?

"A world in which the assets of the 200 richest people are greater than the combined income of the more than 2 billion people at the other end of the economic ladder should give everyone pause," said Jay Mazur in the January 2000 *Foreign Affairs.*

Our neglect means the dispossessed on earth can care nothing for an environment whose plunder by the First World results in so few crumbs for the poor. We insist on this planetwide inequality at our own risk yet continue keeping a distance between ourselves and the world's malnourished billions. That's too bad, because the last time our North American news media was allowed to show us the human suffering caused by our lifestyle, millions of us actually woke up and hit the streets, we marched on the Pentagon, and, for a moment, we protested our own savage innocence, wallowing in guilt. Then the networks removed the human face of war in Vietnam and complacency returned. And all we are really allowed to see anymore is the halftime show at the Superbowl and clever ads for e-commerce and SUVs.

The world's current economic despotism traces its rationale back to Adam Smith. It has survived attacks by Hobson, Marx, the utopian socialists. Bolshevik and Chinese communist revolutions have not long stifled its extraordinary predominance. Modern technology has imbued its imperialist success story with accelerating ecological and human costs that include melting glaciers, destroying the atmosphere, eradicating many of earth's species, leaving billions of humans on the verge of starvation, igniting wars around the globe. Science, which granted capital this power, can now predict the outcome: complete physical and social breakdown of the structures sustaining life. On a planet of finite resources, our growth-oriented, profit-based economic system featuring planned obsolescence and conspicuous consumption is a formula for planetary suicide. So all our protests should begin by stating, "Not capitalism, either."

It's time for a new philosophy.

We need environmentalists—liberation ecologists!—able to speak like George Jackson or Malcolm X and urban activists willing to incorporate John Muir and Rachel Carson. There's no point to North American wilderness without revolution in Guatemala. Reforms buy time, but in the long run they aren't going to work. You can't dismantle the master's house using the master's tools. Our task is to reinvent our economic philosophy and principles to meet the commandments of our *democratic* institutions. That means an end to officially sanctioned selfishness. Forget about private property, we can't afford that anymore. To the extent that our well-being requires the enslavement of others—and most of our conspicuous consumption makes those demands—it is as untenable as Stalinist repression and we don't deserve it.

In *The Closing Circle*, one of the more insightful books written on the subject of our survival, Barry Commoner said that for our ecosystem to endure, the overall social needs of humanity *must* supercede the private interests of producers in a no-growth atmosphere that forgoes "the luxury of tolerating poverty, racial discrimination, and war."

To a liberation ecologist, the most important social, political, and environmental phrase ever uttered is, "All men [women, species] are created equal."

So:

It's a mystery to me how anybody among us develops a social conscience. From early childhood I obviously had an awareness of the unfair world, but monumental events, liberated friends, and a complicated series of personal accidents were required to bludgeon me toward a less selfish worldview. The persuasive national culture shaping all of us kept tugging me in other directions. I don't know if this essay explains why (or even how) I resisted the urge to follow. Certainly I was born into (and then offered additional) privilege such as most of us seldom attain. Obviously, that one punch by Emerick Tedesky is more metaphor than fate . . . but what fun to think it started the process. I know a love of the natural world, my sports heroes, and blues and folk music were important. As were William Floyd, Anatole Le Braz, and a reactionary European grandmother who gave me Spanish and French. By themselves, southern Jim Crow laws should have been enough to make me grow up but weren't. Damon Runyon, rock 'n' roll, and Chicano firefighters out west joined Steinbeck, washing dishes, the Reverend Gary Davis, and a lack of God. And yet . . . and yet it took Alan Howard, Guatemala, Mike Kimmel, *The Master Weaver,* the Vietnam War, marriage to Ruby, and New York publishing cynicism to finally push me *almost* over the edge. Bernard Malamud's exhortation, "In art, no compromise with the ideals of art," gave me encouragement to believe in art when, in my estimation, aesthetics were at their lowest ebb. Having two brothers I loved in the shadow of the Vietnam draft certainly spurred me a few inches farther leftward. As did Diana Oughton and the television news. But my evolution had to be topped off by the entire Taos Valley before I actually broke out of the infantile ignorance imposed by our system into a more conscious and activist life . . . on my terms—as a *writer*—that I had striven for all along.

Yet, what an *effort* was required to finally badger

me irrevocably over the line. Was it worth it to all the forces required to conspire in this project?

I hope so.

Margaret Randall writes, "It is not easy to give up privilege, but it is possible. And ultimately liberating."

I am not as strong as many of the people I admire, and my contradictions make me uncomfortable. Too often I can still feel like an apolitical intellectual . . . or an American child supreme. Yet I've had the good fortune to be inspired by friends moved to act by great feelings of love; philosophically and emotionally they cared about Guatemala. It's amazing to me how I found those friends in a dark century in this culture overly dedicated to ruin. To me, their drive for social and ecological justice has always been the miracle.

And the answer.

Like those flashlight beams in Nicaragua illuminating the dancers.

EPILOGUE

For over forty years the most consistent activity in my life has been writing. Always, late at night, when the meetings or demonstrations or personal brouhahas were over and my family slept, I sat down and wearily produced the pages. More than anything, that work, and its years of continuity, define me. My habits have not changed. Most often I still write in a state of exhaustion, and much of the work suffers accordingly: I publish maybe a fifth of what I produce. Always I keep in mind that old guy, Charles, at the Maple Hill Restaurant in West Hartford, Connecticut, who insisted on the honor due all work. I understand that much of what I do falls short. That in no way diminishes the effort.

As a child I felt I had a gift. I felt I had the gift when I wrote *The Journey* and *Don't Be Forlorn*. I felt I had the gift when I was a strange, isolated young man in my grandmother's Barcelona apartment smoking cigarettes and typing through every night. I felt I had the gift even when it was most threatened, at the height of the Vietnam War, and I was paralyzed by guilt and outrage and a very deep fear that the gift was either not enough or totally irrelevant anyway. Somehow, the gift survived and evolved despite my efforts at sabotage. Underneath, often unbeknownst even to me, I was a maniac for writing. Whatever else my shortcomings, I persisted in what I loved, and what I loved discovered a way to speak beyond the self. As far as I know, that is when art becomes worthwhile.

John Nichols
A PORTRAIT

by Scott Slovic

I am looking at a photograph of my son Jacinto lying
on his back dressed only in short pants, a green
T-shirt, black socks, and old leather hiking boots. The
photo was taken in November 1998, when Jacinto
was eleven years old. He is lying on his back with his
legs kicked up on a Jeffrey pine, relaxed and laughing.
This is his "John Nichols" pose. It's the position John
assumes when he's out roaming the mountains near
his home in Taos, New Mexico, and his arrhythmic
heart acts up, the result of a congenital condition that
helped kill his mother in her twenties, when John was
still a toddler. This is the condition he writes about in
The Last Beautiful Days of Autumn and various other
books and essays, the one that haunts his life and
makes mortality a daily reality. This condition also
helps to infuse his life and work with a devil-may-
care attitude, an extraordinary intensity and joy and
anger. Life is too short and precious to waste.

The uncertainty of living with a serious heart condition would make many people tentative and care-
ful. His shaky heart and a variety of other ailments

111

have had the opposite effect on John Nichols. He exudes energy and curiosity, playful wit and political zeal. The result is a kind of magnetic charisma, an authority that has children (and adults) as far away as the Sierra foothills in Nevada kicking up their heels to savor his stories and reflect on the subversive implications of his social commentary.

The opening line of this *Credo* book raises the work's central issue: "It's a mystery to me," writes John Nichols, "how anybody among us develops a social conscience." Indeed, how does this process occur and why? Why should residents of the United States be concerned with living conditions in the rest of the world or with the status of the environment elsewhere on the planet? Is it enough for people to be self-interested and self-protective, or is life somehow richer and more meaningful if we adopt a perspective of concern and activism? This *Credo* book is about the process by which one American writer developed his own "social conscience," a state of mind that is the crux of his literary work. And by telling his story, Nichols implicitly presents a challenge to the entire field of environmental literature: How can nature writers and ecocritics and their colleagues profess to care about the nonhuman environment without, at the same time, working to ameliorate the lives of fellow human beings?

For Nichols, as the preceding narrative shows, the transformative experience was a journey south of the border to Guatemala in 1964, at the age of twenty-four.

A young literary star, the graduate of Loomis prep school and Hamilton College, he had just sold his first novel, *The Sterile Cuckoo*. He celebrated by spending the five hundred-dollar advance to visit his best friend down in Central America, and the result was "a demarcation . . . an end to innocence . . . my Moby Dick." For the first several drafts, his *Credo* essay was called *Down in Guatemala*, underscoring the importance of Nichols' encounters with the poor of that country and with young American expatriates fueling their compassion—their activist souls—on Guatemala's spirit of revolution and political turbulence. The very words Guatemala and El Salvador were once rallying cries for the radical left in the United States, allusions to loci of human suffering, oppressive governments, and revolutionary passion. But today—today, who cares about Guatemala? Who, especially among our younger generations, even recalls what it once meant to leave behind the relative safety and order of the United States and travel "south of the border"? Remember, it was only a few years before Nichols' revelatory journey that Jack Kerouac had defined the South for a generation in *On the Road* (1955), when his persona Sal Paradise states near the end of the novel:

> I looked over the map: a total of over a thousand miles, mostly Texas, to the border at Laredo, and then another 767 miles through all Mexico to the great city near the cracked Isthmus and Oaxacan heights. I couldn't imagine this trip. It was the most fabulous of all. It was no longer

east-west, but magic *south*. We saw a vision
of the entire Western Hemisphere rockribbing
clear down to Tierra del Fuego and us flying
down the curve of the world into other tropics
and other worlds. "Man, this will finally take us
to IT!" said Dean with definite faith. He tapped
my arm. "Just wait and see. Hoo! Whee!"

Some part of John Nichols, to be sure, was seeking
adventure and excitement during the 1964 trip to
Guatemala. But, as the *Credo* narrative explains, there
was more to this journey than temporary thrills. The
Guatemala trip coincided fatefully with America's increasing involvement in the Vietnam War, another
of the defining political and social phenomena for
Nichols' generation. During his crucial, formative
years following college, Nichols experienced the raw
ferment of a developing nation and the simulta-
neous social upheaval at home over the war in Southeast Asia. These experiences changed his life once
and for all—his entire worldview has been shaped by
these events.

In an early letter during the planning process for
his *Credo* project, Nichols expressed his concern that
he be allowed to express himself freely and to the full
extent of his radical vision. He wrote:

I would be interested in doing an essay for the
Credo Series that you mentioned, providing
that I am free to do it my way, and not subject
to editorial or political constrictions decreed by
the publishers. My experience is that I tend to

take a more radical socio/economic approach to "environmental writing" than many of my cohorts, and I'd hate to run up against policies seeking to moderate, defuse, or otherwise alter my attitude.

The main attraction of this invitation was "the freedom the authors involved would have to make their statement without fear of publishing compromises." What has resulted is an uncensored, extended statement from Nichols about the state of the world and the process by which he himself came to be attuned to environmental and social issues. Milkweed's editors and I have offered gentle tips and suggestions, seeking to limit repetition and occasionally to encourage fuller or clearer explanations. But there has been no attempt to mute or deflect the radical urgency of the writer's message.

In November 1998, John Nichols came to visit the Center for Environmental Arts and Humanities at the University of Nevada, Reno. It was a typical literary junket, the sort of visit John has made to many campuses and towns over the years, involving a few readings from his work, hobnobbing with students and faculty, and some sightseeing. The first evening of his visit, we drove two hours on perilous winter roads to get to Grass Valley, California, where he was scheduled to read in the Literature Alive! series. Winter had just reached the northern Sierra Nevada with a vengeance, and the roads, even Interstate 80, were slick with black ice. I realized during the ride that I had no windshield wiper fluid, so my front windows grew cloudier and cloudier until visibility was just about nil. John rode shotgun, clinging to the door handle and swearing as we tried to make conversation. Finally I stopped at a gas station and cleaned the windows.

Just past Donner Pass, west of Reno, we turned north onto Highway 20, which snakes through the forest to the former mining communities of Nevada City and Grass Valley. Immediately my small Nissan began sliding across the road. There was no traction at all. Other cars were slipping here and there as well. We soon stopped and began trying to put the new chains on my car. I had never done this before, so John crawled around the car and lay the chains next to each tire. Eventually, we got them on. I was thinking all the while about his famous heart condition, the atrial fibrillation he was writing about nearly thirty years ago, the condition that worsened after he had open-heart surgery in 1994. But there he was, en route to a literary evening in the California mountains, throwing chains on his host's car and keeping up a frenzied chatter. Just as we completed our own chain installation, a CalTrans vehicle pulled up behind us. "Too bad—we could have had that guy help us with the chains," I said. Turned out the CalTrans worker didn't know a thing about putting on chains and had stopped to ask us for help. We had to laugh. The irony kept us amused as we poked our way over to Grass Valley, hoping we wouldn't be late for the reading.

The community center on one of the main streets in Grass Valley was packed. The organizers had told me in advance they couldn't predict how many people would show up for the event; they were astounded at the turnout on such a cold November evening. It was par for the course for John Nichols, though. Readers and fans had come out of the proverbial woodwork. Despite the frightening drive, John rose splendidly to the occasion. He sat next to me in an old work coat, wearing a plaid wool shirt, waiting to be introduced by University of California at Davis poet and Gary Snyder scholar Scott Maclean, and then delivered a rousing, rapid-fire presentation that never missed a beat, beginning with an energetic riff from the opening pages of his 1987 novel *American Blood*. After the reading, we declined offers to spend the night in Grass Valley because we had to be back in Reno early the next morning for another event. I praised John's presentation as we walked to the car, wondering how he managed to keep his poise after the harrowing drive. "I'm a pro," he said. "I do this sort of thing all the time. The show must go on." And so it did.

We took a more conservative route back over the mountains to Reno, detouring west toward Auburn and hitting the interstate at a lower elevation. It was after midnight when we finally made it to John's hotel near the campus in Reno. He was up and ready to go early the next morning, despite the previous late night and despite the breach of his normal schedule at home, which has him working all night and finally going to sleep at dawn.

That morning he spoke to my Western Traditions class, a group of 150 undergraduates, about his novel *The Milagro Beanfield War* and the politics of cultural conquest and natural resources in the American Southwest. The students had been studying American history and literature in the course and had just finished reading the novel. I asked John to read a brief passage from the novel that, to his mind, encapsulated the essential point he sought to make in what has become his best-known book among general readers. With that request in mind, he presented the following passage to the students, describing the life of the novel's oldest character, Amarante Córdova:

> All his life Amarante had lived in the shadow of his own death. When he was two days old he caught pneumonia, they gave him up for dead, somehow he recovered. During his childhood he was always sick, he couldn't work like other boys his age. He had rheumatic fever, chicken pox, pneumonia three or four more times, started coughing blood when he was six, was anemic, drowsy all the time, constantly sniffling, weak and miserable, and—everybody thought—dying. At eight he had his tonsils out; at ten, his appendix burst. At twelve he was bitten by a rattlesnake, went into a coma, survived. Then a horse kicked him, breaking all

the ribs on his left side. He contracted tuberculosis. He hacked and stumbled around, hollow-eyed, gaunt and sniffling, and folks crossed themselves, murmuring Hail Marys whenever he staggered into view. At twenty, when he was already an alcoholic, scarlet fever almost laid him in the grave; at twenty-three, malaria looked like it would do the job. Then came several years of amoebic dysentery. After that he was constipated for seventeen months. At thirty, a lung collapsed; at thirty-four, shortly after he became the first sheriff of Milagro, that old devil pneumonia returned for another whack at it, slowed his pulse to almost nothing, but like a classical and very pretty but fainthearted boxer, couldn't deliver the knockout punch. During the old man's forties a number of contending diseases dropped by Amarante's body for a shot at the title. The clap came and went, had a return bout, was counted out. The measles appeared, as did the mumps, but they did not even last a full round. For old time's sake pneumonia made a token appearance, beat its head against the brick wall that evidently lined Amarante's lungs, then waved a white flag and retreated. Blood poisoning blew all his lymph nodes up to the size of golf balls, stuck around for a month, and lost the battle.

John continued for another four paragraphs, telling about Amarante's series of operations in his seventies that led the citizens of Milagro to an "irate, sarcastic, and not a little awed frame of mind" and gave Amarante the nickname "the human zipper." This passage of the novel is comical and fanciful—on the surface it seems to say little about the social and economic conditions of the American Southwest, the region that has been Nichols' home for the past thirty-two years. But Amarante serves as an apt metaphor for Taos and many other Indian and Hispanic communities in the Southwest that have experienced every sort of neglect and outright oppression since the arrival of Europeans, and particularly, in recent decades. And yet, despite rampant poverty and social problems, these communities survive. Like Amarante Córdova, the poor communities of the Southwest defy all expectations of their demise. Many of Nichols' nonfiction writings take a direct, hortatory approach to social and environmental problems. But in his well-known novels, especially *Milagro,* written during the bitter, waning years of the Vietnam War, the predominant strategy is irony and dark humor.

The question of survival, of daily stamina, emerges not only in Nichols' commentaries on the Southwest, but in his own life. The sentence "All his life Amarante had lived in the shadow of his own death" could apply just as easily to John Nichols, whose mother died of a heart infection—endocarditis—when John was two years old. John himself has suffered a variety of ailments and injuries throughout his life, but he seems to delight in pushing himself to and beyond the limits of normal human stamina. He's lived a life of unusual energy and adventure—and has been extraordinarily productive in his professional life, although much of his energy has disappeared into projects, such as unpublished novels and unmade films, that may never be known to the public. Even his daily schedule—which typically begins with his waking up at noon or one in the afternoon, followed by errands and correspondence for a few hours, and then marathon writing and research sessions that last all night until he goes to bed at seven or eight in the morning—has a Herculean feel to it.

The evening of his 1998 visit to Reno, John opened his public reading with a brief rehash of his life, an enumeration of his physical debilities, and a challenge to the listeners. "I was born in 1940, and I've been writing since I was fourteen," he began.

> I've written a lot of books, many of them better than what's been published. And I'm going to offer you a potpourri tonight, readings from various books. We'll see how much stamina you have. I have lots of stamina. I have asthma, I have varicose veins, I have Ménière's disease, I have a condition called "oscillopsia," I've got a rotten heart (I take digitalis every day), I've got a scar from my gullet down to my belly button from open-heart surgery, but digitalis keeps me peppy—so I can outlast any of you all.

And so began the reading, with humor, paradoxical confessions of his own frailty, brash statements of defiance, explanations of his writing aims and processes, and political commentary. To the mixed audience of college students and professors and community members, he announced early on that his primary goal was "to overthrow the capitalist system and replace it with a socialist democracy like that espoused in our own Constitution." Following a brief reading from the prologue to *The Last Beautiful Days of Autumn,* which I had requested, he charged into the passages with which he usually likes to open his public readings: a ten-minute riff from *American Blood,* delivered almost from memory in a rapid drawl. The novel focuses on the experience of a Vietnam vet but actually seeks to illuminate all of American society as a culture rooted in violence: "We stumbled through it in a kind of killing trance. No rhyme, no reason, no front. Went somewhere, got killed, and killed a lot of the diminutive beaners in exchange. Took a hill, suffered great casualties, gave great casualties, and departed next day, never to return." Jocular and friendly, Nichols uses his natural rapport with audiences, and with individuals he meets, as a way to present his genuinely radical message about the ills of American society and all capitalist societies.

More recently, on May 13, 2000, he was given an honorary degree at the University of New Mexico. Nichols prepared a two-page speech in which he celebrated the working people of the world and shared the honor of the special degree with them. Essentially, the five-minute presentation recapitulated the story offered in this *Credo* book. "When I graduated from college thirty-eight years ago," he began,

I had to start over, as you most certainly will, learning everything from scratch. My formal education had prepared me to succeed in our culture, but not to really understand the planet or to sympathize with it in a compassionate manner. I knew very little about love or work or the tragedy of environment and people under attack by material development. You could say I was probably like most of you: a real *sábe-lotodo, compréndelonada.*

My disillusion with America began two years after college on a trip to Guatemala in 1964, when I was appalled to see how our economic policies created so much Latin misery. My disillusion climaxed in the fires of Vietnam, which almost destroyed me, not because I am a Vietnam veteran, but because for nine years I organized in appalled astonishment against a devastating war that my misguided country simply would not end. . . .

But the key point of his speech is not the malevolence of the social and economic forces that lead to war and oppression. The focus is on the author's love for the everyday heroism of the working class:

When I came to New Mexico in 1969, this state gave me back hope, but not for the reasons you might think. Being the poorest state in our nation allies us intimately with most of the rest of the people on earth. Folks I love and have been inspired by in this place are the salt of the earth. Rarely do they receive accolades or even

123 ❧

modest recognition. Many kill themselves for minimum wages, and they do not have the safety nets of retirement pensions or health care insurance plans. They defend the acequias, pick the vegetables that go on our tables, and build the houses we live in. Their jobs can be deadening or dangerous, and higher education for them is often out of reach.

But they make the world work, and they labor so hard on behalf of everyone.

An inveterate reader and aficionado of films, Nichols referred the graduates to the movie *Salt of the Earth,* made years ago in Silver City, New Mexico. And he celebrated the "remarkable sense of humor" of his working-class friends and neighbors in Taos. Speaking in a playful combination of English and Spanish, he lauded the common people and poked fun at the military-industrial complex, particularly the community of Los Alamos, which was battling extraordinary wildfires at the time of the ceremony. "My neighbors," he claimed, "are the indefatigable majority on earth, and they gave me my novels and the other books I've published and all the films I've worked on."

Much of the important information about John Nichols' life and work is available in his autobiographical *Credo* essay, particularly the story of his family background on Long Island and in Europe and the details of his political awakening. There is also ample biographical information in Carl Shirley's article in *Dictionary of Literary Biography: Yearbook 1982* and in Peter Wild's 1986 pamphlet on Nichols for the Western Writers Series. Nichols himself has written a number of autobiographical essays, such as his self-portrait for the *Contemporary Authors Autobiography Series* and many of the pieces collected in the recent volume *Dancing on the Stones: Selected Essays*. John's reflections on his father's life and their relationship were published in a 1997 essay in *Audubon* magazine, just months before his father died. The piece focuses on his father's interest in birds and his sharing of that interest with John and his brothers.

Some of Nichols' identity as a writer—both his early impetus to go into this field and his sense of working in a family tradition today—is rooted in the fact that his mother was related to a significant French literary figure. Likewise, his lifelong fascination with the natural world is firmly rooted in a sense of family tradition. Not only was his father a gifted naturalist, but his grandfather and namesake, John T. Nichols, served as curator of fishes at the American Museum of Natural History in New York City and founded the American Society of Ichthyologists and Herpetologists (ASIH) and its journal, *Copeia*. Having made such an issue of Nichols' political stance earlier in this portrait, it is only fair at this point to emphasize the centrality of the natural world to his life and work. In June 1991, John delivered the keynote address, entitled "What Is a Naturalist, Anyway?" at the seventy-fifth annual meeting of ASIH at the Natural History Museum in New York, a talk that was later published in *Copeia, Natural History Magazine,* and *Dancing on the Stones.* The *Natural History* article includes a photo of John and his grandfather taken at the family's Mastic, New York, home in 1941. Another copy of the photo appeared years earlier in *The Last Beautiful Days of Autumn,* with the caption "My grandfather, John T. Nichols, passed it on." The sense of legitimacy received through family lineage is very clear. What's also clear, from the 1991 essay, is that Nichols identifies himself as a naturalist and sees this perspective as fundamentally consonant with social and political stances articulated in this *Credo* essay. This is how he defines "naturalist":

> I would propose that a naturalist is a person whose curiosity is boundless. He or she is interested in kinkajous and sticklebacks, in astronomy, French wine, magpies, baseball, prairie rattlesnakes, quantum mechanics, corn on the cob, great sperm whales, and even Bolsheviks and hummingbirds. A naturalist is a person who tries to delight in everything, is in love with the whole of life, and hopes to walk in harmony across this earth. A naturalist might also be a lunatic like myself who would like to overthrow a capitalist system based on planned obsolescence and conspicuous consumption because he believes that is a formula for planetary suicide. . . .

> In short, a naturalist chooses not to be anthropocentric, believing, rather, that every thing has an equal right to life on earth—whether it's an elephant, a peasant from El Salvador, an African cichlid, or a tiny bacterium.

Given the opportunity to reflect on the life and work of his grandfather, John used the occasion as a forum to espouse an entire worldview that begins with his grandfather's interest in the natural world but moves well beyond a strict focus on fish, reptiles, and the entire realm of traditional natural history. This is important to keep in mind when thinking about the rather encompassing approach to nature, community, and the writing life adopted in this *Credo* book.

Nichols' first novel appeared in 1965, and that year he also sold *The Wizard of Loneliness*, another novel. He did not publish another book until *The Milagro Beanfield War* in 1974. *Milagro* received meager attention initially. However, John sold the film option for the book, and this income kept his family going. The critic Bruce-Novoa would suggest provocatively in his 1990 book *Retrospace: Collected Essays on Chicano Literature, Theory and History* that *Milagro* so effectively expresses the themes of Chicano experience that, if one could accept the fact that the author was not born to Mexican parents and had simply "learned" the culture, "we would be faced with another situation, intolerable for many Chicanos, in which our best novelist could well be John Nichols."

The Magic Journey, the second volume in what

would become Nichols' New Mexico Trilogy, appeared in 1978. Of the three novels in the series, Nichols has stated, *"Magic Journey* is by far the most important to me, a novel into which I poured my entire life, my politics, my vision of the world. Compared to the others, it is a difficult read. Yet if anything I have written lasts beyond me, I fervently hope it will be that book." The novel is set in a New Mexico town called Chamisaville, and the story takes place between the Great Depression and the 1970s. Picking up on some of the themes in *Milagro,* the second novel in the trilogy tells the story of development in what had been a small, sleepy town, with businessmen and politicians in cahoots to make money off of tourists, exploiting the local Chicano population in the process.

Two new books were published in 1979: *If Mountains Die* and the novel *A Ghost in the Music.* The novel had actually started out thirteen years earlier as *A Big Diaphanous Wild Man. A Ghost in the Music* extends Nichols' interest in the bizarre and tender complexities of love, established years earlier with *The Sterile Cuckoo.* The new book tells the story of middle-aged, third-rate movie jack-of-all-trades Bart Darling (producer, actor, director, and stuntman), who enlists his illegitimate son, Marcel Thompson, to help him lure back Lorraine, the latest in a string of wives and lovers. The novelistic exploration—and often critique—of romantic relationships would continue eventually with *An Elegy for September* (1992) and *Conjugal Bliss* (1994). *If Mountains Die,* on the other hand, is a nonfiction book that tells the story of Nichols' arrival in northern New Mexico and his passionate concern for the future of the region, including the preservation of both local culture and natural beauty. Illuminating Nichols' prose are Bill Davis' sublime landscape photographs.

Costa-Gavras hired John to work on the screenplay for the film *Missing* in 1980, and with this project Nichols' film career started in earnest. *Missing* would eventually be nominated for four Academy Awards and win the award for best adapted screenplay, but Nichols was arbitrated out of a credit by the Writers Guild Union. He worked on two other films, *Warday* and *The Magic City,* with Costa-Gavras between 1981 and 1984, and also began tinkering with a screenplay for *Milagro* for producer Moctesuma Esparza. Within a few years he was working on a screenplay for Karel Reisz as well. By 1984, Robert Redford had become involved in the *Milagro* film project, which appeared in theaters in 1988. As Nichols explains in a recent article called "To Make a Long Story Short," an account of his work in the film industry, his major contribution to the movie version of *Milagro* was his recommendation that 80 percent of the narrative and 90 percent of the characters be thrown out and that the story be presented from the point of view of a single character, Joe Mondragon, "the feisty little guy who illegally irrigates a bean field, thus opening the floodgates of state retribution, which is promptly answered by indigenous revolution." More recent film endeavors have included

Midnight Return, a sequel to the 1978 Alan Parker/ Oliver Stone film *Midnight Express.* John labored for three years, 1996 to 1999, to get this script into shape, but the project is still languishing without a director. During the past few years, he has fed his interest in leftist politics and radical history by writing *Che and Fidel,* a screenplay about his heroes Che Guevara and Fidel Castro. Despite the fact that few of his scripts have actually made it to the screen, Nichols notes "the economic punchline . . . is that I have always been paid for my failures: that is, I never wrote a screenplay on spec." In other words, much of his literary work over the years—the published projects, the unpublished manuscripts, and the pieces written for good causes and no money—has been funded by writing for the movies.

Even as John began his film career with Costa-Gavras in the early 1980s, he was still actively working on fiction, nonfiction, and his new passion, landscape photography. The last book in the New Mexico Trilogy, *The Nirvana Blues,* came out in 1981. This bleak but typically playful novel seems to cancel any hope for the survival of traditional Chicano culture in New Mexico. The fictional town of Chamisaville has become Mecca West, the place to go for "flower children, teeny-Bs, acid heads, burly bikers, road and speed freaks, stone-cold dopers, flatulent gurus, Edgar Cayce disciples, orgone idiots, hang-glider enthusiasts, and other exotic breeds." The novel's main characters, Joe Miniver and Eloy Irribarren, perish at the book's conclusion. But in the epilogue, Joe's soul hijacks a flying machine piloted by an angel named Lorin and bails out over Cuba, where "the sweetness of a fresh and real start infused his spectral protoplasm." Although the novel is unrelenting in its critique of capitalist American society, the story expresses a dark optimism about human nature, given certain fundamental revampings of social and economic systems.

Nichols' first public display of photography occurred with the 1982 publication of *The Last Beautiful Days of Autumn,* a book that combined his lush color photos of northern New Mexico with autobiographical essays about the first decade of his life there. As was the case with *If Mountains Die,* the primary mood of the new nonfiction book was nostalgic and cautionary, celebrating the beauty of the region and warning that the land and people are both threatened by progress. By the mid-1980s, he had begun working on what he has since suggested are two of his favorite literary projects: the nonfiction book *On the Mesa* and the novel *American Blood. On the Mesa,* which appeared in 1986, is an essay inspired by a puddle of water surrounded by three hundred square yards of sagebrush, located just west of Taos. The author himself thinks of the stockpond as his own desert version of Thoreau's Walden Pond. *American Blood* came out in 1987. Though this was first intended to be a large historical novel based on years of research about the rise of industrial capitalism in this country, Nichols eventually published a slender version of the epic story he had planned to tell, which focused on the central metaphor of violence under-lying our civilization.

Married for the second time in 1985, but divorced in 1989, Nichols satirized this exciting but volatile marriage in the novel *Conjugal Bliss*. Meanwhile, his 1966 novel, *The Wizard of Loneliness,* was being made into a movie in Bristol, Vermont, so John went back to New England to watch the filming. He began working on a novel called *Democracy in Action* in 1988, a book that will be published in 2001 with the revised title *The Voice of the Butterfly.*

The Sky's the Limit: A Defense of the Earth marked a new direction in Nichols' environmental writing when it appeared in 1990. This book combines Nichols' color landscape photos with dire page-long statements about environmental degradation. His extended introduction to the book explains the purpose of this "exercise in antonyms":

> I cannot look at a lovely scene without being aware of the bulldozers just out of frame, waiting to plunder. There is no such thing, anymore, as an apolitical landscape photograph. All environment is threatened; all air is poisoned. Hence the more unspoiled a moment appears, the more intensely I fear its pending destruction.

Nichols published another photo-essay combination in 1993 called *Keep It Simple*. This book has a pressing personal dimension to it. He describes his efforts to simplify his own life in the interest of health and peace of mind, realizing at the same time that there's little a single person can do amid a culture bent on speed and consumption. Meanwhile, his own life, though perhaps moderately simplified in comparison with previous hectic years, continued to be busy and full. The novel *An Elegy for September* appeared in 1992, telling the story of a middle-aged writer who has an affair with a young fan.

Nichols was working on the screenplay *Amazonia* for Ridley Scott, teaching creative writing workshops at the University of New Mexico, drafting *Conjugal Bliss,* and taking flamenco guitar lessons in 1992 and 1993, despite the scare caused by serious heart fibrillation and congestive heart failure due to a prolapsed mitral valve. Finally, on May 4, 1994, after doing a book tour for *Conjugal Bliss* despite the heart problems, John underwent open-heart surgery to have the faulty valve repaired. He gradually regained his health and busied himself with new and ongoing projects, supported by many friends, his children Luke and Tania, and their mother Ruby, who occasionally visits from Albuquerque.

When a friend gave Nichols his first computer in 1993, the writer typed up years' worth of miscellaneous speeches and essays, making it possible to pull together the essay collection *Dancing on the Stones,* which appeared in 2000. As he approached his sixtieth birthday on July 23, 2000, he drafted another novel called *Duende*. When not toiling at various projects or traveling around the country to rouse the rabble at readings and commencements, John loves hiking in the high mountains, even reaching the summit of Wheeler Peak, the tallest mountain in New Mexico at more than thirteen thousand feet, several times in recent years despite his assorted health problems. A marvel of energy, vision, and sheer joy, there is no sign that John Nichols is slowing down at the end of six decades.

On July 25, two days after John's sixtieth birthday, my friend Susie and I showed up to spend the day with him and get a feel for how he lives. We rendezvoused at the Taos Plaza, roughly a quarter mile from the small adobe house where John lives mainly by himself, sometimes sharing the place with his son Luke. John waved from his 1993 Dodge Shadow as he pulled into the square, crowded with summer tourists. "I'm not wearing my teeth," he quickly said, explaining the gap in his smile. "Got this chronic bone infection in my upper jaw that's been driving me crazy—wearing the bridge just makes it feel worse." Unshaven, dressed in gray khakis with the cuffs rolled up, a blue-and-pink striped dress shirt that hung past his waist, plastic-rimmed glasses, and taped-together Saucony sneakers, John was clearly unconcerned with appearances. The scar from his 1994 surgery was visible above his top shirt button. Despite the bone infection, pain medication, and antibiotics, he was in good spirits, talkative as ever.

We followed him back to his place, winding through narrow streets, past gentrified adobes and plain, working-class houses with multiple cars and run-down trucks parked out front. His home is a gray, four-room adobe building with a dirt driveway, four apple trees, a plot of sunflower plants, and a wooden shed he built to hold his research books. Inside, John's bedroom is a darkened library, with two file cabinets, shelves of well-used books on every side, and a stack of a dozen boxes containing his father's archives. Even the small bathroom has bookshelves in it. The bedroom leads directly into John's living room/workspace, where his computer sits at a narrow desk next to a TV and VCR, surrounded by more bookshelves and eight four-drawer file cabinets. Even the simple kitchen adjoining the study has bookshelves and piles of papers on the table. A bare lightbulb hangs from the center of the room. The only other room is a small portal sleeping area that extends from the kitchen—where Luke crashes when he's inclined.

John immediately began to show us what he'd been working on the previous night, the boxes of old correspondence to and from his father, dating back to the 1930s. The entire Nichols family, it's clear, has an astounding mania for collecting things, from old letters and manuscripts to bugs and birds. After touring the research shed and sifting through some sample files in the cabinets distributed throughout the little house, even taking a peek at the first letter ever written by five-year-old John Nichols to his grandmother (and tucked safely in a folder of its own), we climbed into his Shadow for a tour of the neighborhood. First stop was Hinds & Hinds Budget

Storage, a few blocks from home, where John has three storage units loaded with neatly shelved drafts of published and unpublished manuscripts, boxes of books, and most of his father's belongings recently hauled over from Smithville, Texas. In one unit there were two entire walls of manuscripts, dozens of drafts, it seemed, for each of the volumes in the New Mexico Trilogy. All of this work was produced on a small, manual typewriter, which John held up for a photograph, smiling sans front teeth. Another novel, *An American Child Supreme,* went through some thirty-five drafts between 1966 and 1975 before the author gave up on it—but the manuscripts are now neatly stacked at Hinds & Hinds. Someday these materials will be housed in the special collection at a university library, perhaps at the University of New Mexico, but for now this is all a private research stash, as John works on a memoir about his family, tentatively called *Goodbye, Monique* (referring to his mother).

Billowy clouds began to collect in the sky over Taos as we made our way next to Upper Ranchitos Road to take a look at the adobe where John and his family first lived after arriving from New York in 1969. Our guide kept up a happy monologue as we drove past the overgrown fields and luxuriant cotton-woods along Upper Ranchitos. "This is where Steve Mondragón's pig got out and gave me the idea for the pig in *Milagro.* Look at these neat little neighbor-hoods. You can tell which houses have been gentri-fied and which are still lived in by locals. That's where my buddy Alfred Peralta, owner of the laundromat, lives. . . ." The community came to life through John's stories and the names of people and places. We stopped and he clambered down into the Pacheco ditch, the acequia on which he once served as one of three commissioners, showing us the wooden headgate that gave him the idea thirty years ago of building an entire epic narrative on the theme of locals and developers fighting for precious water.

Back home, we collected our backpacks and some snacks for a late afternoon hike near Wheeler Peak, north of town. John made us a lunch of yellow potato bread, mayonnaise sprinkled with pepper, and slices of American cheese. Then he entertained with two quick bluesy songs on Luke's Stratocaster electric guitar before we headed out. It was four-thirty in the afternoon. After a twenty-minute ride, occasionally through driving rain, we caught the trail near the Taos Ski Valley, 10,210 feet above sea level. We would hike uphill in the direction of Williams Lake, below the gray-green Wheeler massif. Although he needed to stop and catch his breath every five minutes or so, John maintained the nonstop conversation, talking about his dad and his brothers, about his approach to writing and the business of literature and film. "When you organize material, it becomes valuable and accessible," he explained when I asked him about his willingness to sort through the mountains of old family papers that awaited him at home. John and Susie tried to identify plants as we hiked into the deepening dusk. Oshá, larkspur, wild geranium, harebell, bluebell, deer's ears, corn lilies, fleabane, daisies.

We debated about tree identification based on bark texture. "This one's bark is worse than its bite," he quipped. It took us more than an hour to get to Williams Lake, and night was quickly falling. Still, John patiently posed for an "a-fib picture," lying on his back and kicking his feet up on a rock—a photo for Jacinto in exchange for the picture of my son in a similar posture back home in Nevada, given to John for his recent birthday. We hiked for another half hour, clambering across rocks to a lookout point below the distant summit of Wheeler. "Let's contemplate eternity for a few minutes," he suggested, sipping from the reused plastic water bottle tucked in his front shirt pocket.

It was completely dark by the time we returned to John's car. After driving a few minutes on the winding mountain road, he handed the wheel over to me. His night vision's not what it used to be. We made our way back to Taos and found a simple Mexican eatery on the main drag. Over dinner John grilled Susie about her work with international students at the University of Nevada. "You mean, you actually go out and *recruit* students overseas?" His curiosity was intense. I'd already finished my meal, and I couldn't help noticing the relish with which John polished off his taco, enchilada, tamale, rice, and beans, pouring honey over everything, washing it down with a second beer. He'd been talking steadily since early afternoon, explaining his work, his vision for the world, and teasing me about this portrait I'm supposed to write about his whirlwind of a life. I found myself thinking of Thoreau's wish to "live deep and suck out all the marrow of life"—his splendid exhortation, to himself and his readers, to celebrate life and the simple thrill of being in the world. Reading John Nichols' many books, and observing him during public performances and in the context of his daily life, I have the feeling Thoreau would have approved of this energetic, wacky, passionate man. "L'chaim," John Nichols often signs his correspondence. To life, indeed.

Bibliography of John Nichols' Work

by John Nichols and Patrick Barron

BOOKS

The Voice of the Butterfly. San Francisco: Chronicle Books, 2001.

Dancing on the Stones: Selected Essays. Albuquerque: University of New Mexico Press, 2000.

Armageddon and New Mexico: Writing for Fun and Profit in the Poorest State in America. Santa Fe, N. Mex.: Rydal Press, 2000 (limited edition).

Conjugal Bliss: A Comedy of Martial Arts. New York: Henry Holt, 1994. New York: Ballantine, 1995 (paperback edition). Lisbon: Circulo de Leitores, 1995 (Portuguese edition). São Paulo, Brazil: Editora Best Seller, 1995 (Portuguese book club edition).

An Elegy for September. New York: Henry Holt, 1992. New York: Ballantine, 1993 (paperback edition).

Keep It Simple: A Defense of the Earth. New York: W. W. Norton, 1992.

The Sky's the Limit: A Defense of the Earth. New York: W. W. Norton, 1990.

A Fragile Beauty: John Nichols' Milagro Country. Salt Lake City, Utah: Peregrine Smith, 1987.

American Blood. New York: Henry Holt, 1987. New York: Ballantine, 1988 (paperback edition). London: Paladin, 1990 (British edition). Arhus: Klim, 1989 (Danish edition). München: Ernst Kabel, 1990 (German edition). Bergisch Gladbach: Bastei Lubbe, 1993 (German edition). Bussum: Het Wereldvenster, 1989 (Dutch edition).

On the Mesa. Salt Lake City, Utah: Peregrine Smith, 1986. Santa Fe, N. Mex.: Ancient City Press, 1995 (paperback edition with new foreword).

The Last Beautiful Days of Autumn. New York: Holt, Rinehart and Winston, 1982. Santa Fe, N. Mex.: Ancient City Press, 2000 (paperback edition with new foreword).

The Nirvana Blues. New York: Holt, Rinehart and Winston, 1981. New York: Ballantine, 1983 (paperback edition). Bergisch Gladbach: Bastei Lubbe, 1993 (German paperback edition). München: Ernst Kabel, 1991, 1996 (German cloth and paperback editions). New York: Ballantine, 1996 (paperback edition). New York: Henry Holt, 2000 (paperback edition).

A Ghost in the Music. New York: Holt, Rinehart and Winston, 1979. New York: Quality Paperback Book Club, 1979 (book club edition). New York: W. W. Norton, 1996 (paperback edition).

If Mountains Die: A New Mexico Memoir. New York: Alfred A. Knopf, 1979. New York: W. W. Norton, 1996 (paperback edition).

The Magic Journey. New York: Holt, Rinehart and Winston, 1978. New York: Holt, Rinehart and

Winston, 1978 (paperback edition). New York: Pocket Books, 1979 (paperback edition). New York: Ballantine, 1983 (paperback edition). München: Ernst Kabel, 1988 (German edition). Bergisch Gladbach: Bastei Lubbe, 1992 (German edition). Poznań: Zysk i S-ka, 1999 (Polish edition). New York: Henry Holt, 2000 (paperback edition).

The Milagro Beanfield War. New York: Holt, Rinehart and Winston, 1974. London: Andre Deutsch, 1977 (British edition). New York: Ballantine, 1976 (paperback edition). London: Arrow Books Limited/Arena, 1987 (British paperback edition). Barcelona: Seix Barral, 1988 (Spanish edition). Barcelona: Circulo de Lectores (Spanish book club edition). São Paulo, Brazil: Editora Best Seller, 1988 (Portuguese edition). Paris: Londreys, 1988 (French edition). München: Ernst Kabel, 1987 (German edition). Bergisch Gladbach: Bastei Lubbe, 1988 (German paperback edition). Bussum: Het Wereldvenster, 1988 (Dutch edition). Milan: Longanesi, 1988 (Italian edition). Arhus: Klim, 1988 (Danish edition). New York: Henry Holt, 1994 (facsimile edition). Poznań: Zysk i S-ka, 1997 (Polish edition). New York: Henry Holt, 2000 (paperback edition).

The Wizard of Loneliness. New York: G. P. Putnams, 1966. London: Heinemann, 1966 (British edition). New York: Signet, 1967 (paperback edition). Warsaw: Kik, 1970 (Polish edition). New York: Pocket, 1979 (paperback edition). Vianen: Uitgeverij Areopagus, 1970 (Dutch edition). New York: W. W. Norton, 1988 (paperback edition).

The Sterile Cuckoo. New York: David McKay, 1965.
New York: Avon, 1966 (paperback edition). New
York: Literary Guild, 1965 (book club edition).
London: Heinemann, 1965 (British edition).
München: R. Piper and Company Verlag, 1966
(German edition). Leiden: A. W. Sijthoff, 1966
(Dutch edition). Milan: Bompiani, 1970 (Italian
edition). London: Pan Books, 1967 (British paper-
back edition). Tokyo: Hayakawa, 1970 (Japanese
edition). Rio de Janeiro, Brazil: Dis. Record, 1970
(Portuguese edition). New York: Pocket Books,
1979 (paperback edition). New York: W. W.
Norton, 1995 (paperback edition).

UNCOLLECTED ESSAYS AND STORIES

"Read Free or Die." *Book Talk* 29, no. 1 (October
2000). Reprinted in *Librarians' Guild
Communicator* 34, no. 4 (July/August 2000).

"Sin Agua No Hay Vida." *Water* Exhibition Catalog
(Magnifico and the Albuquerque Museum)
(August 18, 2000).

"On That First Trip to the West." *Arizona Republic*
(July 16, 2000).

"Multiple Histories of Youth." *Islas En El Tiempo:
Alex Harris* (IVAM Centre Julio Gonzalez, Valencia,
Spain) (July 2000).

"Internet Commentary." *Corrales Comment* 19,
no. 9 (June 24, 2000).

"Synopsis of My Great, Made-for-Movies, New
Novel" and "A Monument to Imperialism."
Inside/Outside 3, no. 1 (January 2000).

"Essential Readings." *Workbook* 24, no. 4 (Winter 1999/2000).

"Opening the Door to a Hopeful Future." *New Mexico Planning Association Newsletter* (December 1999).

"Negative Realities We Can't Afford to Ignore." *Summit Free Press* (December 1999).

"Into Pretty Thin Air." *Horse Fly* (November 15, 1999).

"Hiking Devisadero." *New Mexico Magazine* 77, no. 3 (March 1999).

"Conscience and Community." *Summit Free Press* (February 1999).

"Taos Mesa: Showtime Im Niemandsland." *Geo: Canyonlands USA* (Hamburg, Germany) (December 1998).

"Eulogy for Mike Kimmel." *Fly Rod and Reel* (July/August 1998).

"What Is to Be Done?" *Summit Free Press* (July 1998).

"Milagro: Twenty-Five Years Later." *Taos Talking Pictures* (official program) (April 16, 1998).

"Dancing on the Stones." *Audubon* 100, no. 2 (March/April 1998).

"Clouds." *New Mexico Magazine* 76, no. 3 (March 1998).

"Simply Living." *Hemp Times* 2, no. 1 (January 1998).

"A Man for All Seasons." *Audubon* 99, no. 6 (November/December 1997).

"A Traffic Violation." *ISLE: Interdisciplinary Studies in Literature and Environment* 4, no. 1 (1997).

"A September Song." *New Mexico Magazine* 74, no. 8 (September 1996).

"Rain." *Sanctuary* 35, no. 5 (May/June 1996).

"A Traffic Violation" and "Our Scam Explained." *Colorado Springs Independent* 4, no. 15 (April 10, 1996).

"Owed to the Typewriter." *Book Talk* (1996).

"How to Succeed As a Writer . . . in 1,256,347 Lessons." *Bloomsbury Review* 15, no. 2 (March/April 1995).

"Pipe Dreams in a Novel Mode." *Book Talk* 24, no. 1 (January 1995).

"A Habit of Seeing." *New Mexico Magazine* 72, no. 9 (September 1994).

"Milagro Madness: How An Unsuccessful Cult Novel Became an Unsuccessful Cult Film in Only 14 Years, 11 Nervous Breakdowns, and $20 Million." *Albuquerque Monthly* (March 1994).

"On the Mesa." *North Fork Valley Chronicle* 1, no. 3 (April 1993).

"John Nichols . . . on Writing." *Journeys—A Literary Magazine* 2, no. 1 (Spring 1993).

"What Is a Naturalist, Anyway?" *Natural History* 101, no. 11 (November 1992).

"The Holiness of Water." *New Mexico Magazine* 70, no. 7 (July 1992).

"An Elegy for September." *Playboy* 39, no. 6 (June 1992).

"Can a Yuppie Marxist Really Find Happiness in the Land of Entrapment?" *El Palacio* 97, no. 2 (Museum of New Mexico)(Spring/Summer 1992).

"What Is a Naturalist, Anyway?" *Copeia* (Journal of the American Society of Ichthyologists and Herpetologists), no. 4 (December 13, 1991).

"A Bright Edge of the World." *Outside* 16, no. 10 (October 1991).

"In Defense of the Earth." *Esquire,* no. 8 (Japanese Edition) (July 1991).

"Clear Views: The Modern Mesa May Soon Vanish." *Elle* 6, no. 1, no. 61 (September 1990).

"The Need for a Triple Soul." *Taos Times* (March 23, 1990).

"Garbage." *Taos Review,* no. 3 (1990).

"Personal Territory." *American Photographer* 23, no. 2 (August 1989).

"Eulogy for Ed Abbey." *Tucson Weekly* (April 5, 1989).

"Ask Edgar Cayce." *Taos Review*, premier issue (1989).

"Snow Job." *Film Comment* 24, no. 5 (October 1988).

"Milagro: Fragile Bellezza del Nuovo Messico." *Epoca,* no. 1967 (June 1988).

"Greetings from Europe: John Nichols Travels on $600, 2 Pairs of Shoes, 12 Aspirins, 4 Valium and 3 Laxatives a Day." *Albuquerque Journal, Impact Magazine* 6, no. 37 (April 12, 1988).

"For Jim Sagel." *Ventana Abierta: Revista Latina* (Center for Chicano Studies, University of California-Santa Barbara) 2, no. 5 (Fall 1998).

"A Fragile Beauty." *Albuquerque Journal, Impact Magazine* 10, no. 53 (October 20, 1987).

"Landscapes of the Universe." *Mass Journal* (New Mexico School of Architecture) 13, nos. 5 and 6 (Fall 1987).

"Behind the Scenes: Bob and the Beanstalk." *American Film* 24, no. 5 (May 1987).

"An Exquisite Place to Start." *Hamilton '62 Twenty-Fifth Reunion Yearbook* (Hamilton College) (April 8, 1987).

"The Stock Pond." *Albuquerque Journal, Impact Magazine* 9, no. 21 (March 11, 1986).

"Suicide Slide, Rope, and Rattlesnake Turn Serious Author into Happy Fisherman." *Santa Fe Lifestyle* 1, no. 1 (Summer 1985).

"Quest for Wide Vistas." *Dallas Times Herald* (July 8, 1984).

"After the Triumph—Nicaragua: Impressions of a Revolution in Progress." *Albuquerque Journal, Impact Magazine* 7, no. 19 (February 28, 1984).

"John Nichols' *On the Mesa*." *Albuquerque Journal, Impact Magazine* 7, no. 13 (January 17, 1984).

"An Evening with a Tranquility Junkie." *Taos News,* Arts section (October 1, 1983).

With photos by Jay Dusard. "Living Portrait of the North American Cowboy." *American West* 20, no. 5 (September/October 1983).

"Rafting the Rio." *Albuquerque Journal, Impact Magazine* 6, no. 37 (June 28, 1983).

"Short Season." *Outside* 8, no. 4 (June 1983).

"A Forgotten Fact Opens Fishing Trip to Danger." *Dallas Times Herald* (January 2, 1983).

"The Last Beautiful Days of Autumn." *Mother Jones* 7, no. 9 (November 1982).

"*Missing* Screenplay Credit." *Cineaste* 12, no. 2 (1982).

Translation by Rini Templeton. "Una Nueva Era McCarthy a la Vuelta de la Esquina." *El Dia: Vocero del Pueblo Mexicano* (August 2, 1981).

"A Day in the Barrel." *Taos' Rio Grande Magazine* 3, no. 3 (Summer 1981).

"Showdown in Ensenada: One Family's Fight for Its Land." *Taos Magazine* 2, no. 4 (Fall 1980).

"Hitch-Hikers." *Taos Magazine* 2, no. 3 (Summer 1980).

"Craft: A Return to Self Reliance." *New Mexico Craft* (May 1980).

"The Lure of the Rio Grande." *Rocky Mountain Magazine* (April 1980).

"No Rhyme, No Reason." *TriQuarterly* 48 (Spring 1980).

"Calaveras." *Rocky Mountain Magazine* (October 1979).

"Taos Paseo." *Rocky Mountain Magazine* (June 1979).

"If Mountains Die." *Taos Magazine* 1, no. 3 (March/April 1979).

"Neighbors" and "Politics." *New America* 3, no. 3 (Spring 1979).

"New Water Problems Loom for Chicano Farmers." *Race Relations Reporter Newsletter* 5, no. 15 (August 12, 1974).

"To Save a Dying Culture." *Race Relations Reporter* 5, no. 13 (July 1974).

"If They Won't Take a Grasshopper the Fish Ain't Biting." *Outdoor Reporter* 10, no. 4 (June 1974).

"A Tinkertoy Approach to Politics." *New Mexico Review* 4, no. 11 (November 1972).

"Accidents Will Happen." *New Mexico Review* 4, no. 11 (November 1972).

"Better Dead than Waterbed." *New Mexico Review* 4, no. 11 (November 1972).

"Boettcher's Sprytron." *New Mexico Review* 4, no. 11 (November 1972).

"Every Five Days a Hiroshima Bomb Is Dropped on Vietnam." *New Mexico Review* 4, no. 11 (November 1972).

"Indian Camp Dam—No, but Maybe." *New Mexico Review* 4, no. 11 (November 1972).

"New Mexico Jails: Not Even a Rat Can Stand Them." *New Mexico Review* 4, no. 11 (November 1972).

"People Against Pete." *New Mexico Review* 4, no. 11 (November 1972).

"Trout Times Infinity." *Southwest Magazine* 1, no. 2 (November 1972).

"A Blot on the Nation." *New Mexico Review* 4, no. 10 (October 1972).

"George McGovern in Española: Still a Human Being." *New Mexico Review* 4, no. 10 (October 1972).

"Indian Camp Dam: The Hunting of the Snark." *New Mexico Review* 4, no. 10 (October 1972).

"La Clinica de la Gente." *New Mexico Review* 4, no. 10 (October 1972).

"Of Mice and Jet Fighters, Buzz Saws and Dead Roadrunners." *New Mexico Review* 4, no. 10 (October 1972).

"What About the Indians?" *New Mexico Review* 4, no. 10 (October 1972).

"A Town Changes Its Name." *New Mexico Review* 4, nos. 8–9 (September 1972).

"Adios, Montana and Wyoming?" *New Mexico Review* 4, nos. 8–9 (September 1972).

"All's Moot That Ends Moot." *New Mexico Review* 4, nos. 8–9 (September 1972).

"Convention Violence." *New Mexico Review* 4, nos. 8–9 (September 1972).

"Jane Fonda in Hanoi." *New Mexico Review* 4, nos. 8–9 (September 1972).

"King Endorses McGovern." *New Mexico Review* 4, nos. 8–9 (September 1972).

"Meanwhile, on the Other Side of the World." *New Mexico Review* 4, nos. 8–9 (September 1972).

"No Posey Pluckers." *New Mexico Review* 4, nos. 8–9 (September 1972).

"Politics New Mexico Style." *New Mexico Review* 4, nos. 8–9 (September 1972).

"Quotations from Chairman Dave." *New Mexico Review* 4, nos. 8–9 (September 1972).

"Rural Schools: Going Down Angry." *New Mexico Review* 4, nos. 8–9 (September 1972).

"Ships That Pass in the Night." *New Mexico Review* 4, nos. 8–9 (September 1972).

"Stealing Water the 'Right' Way." *New Mexico Review* 4, nos. 8–9 (September 1972).

"To Bee or Not to Bee." *New Mexico Review* 4, nos. 8–9 (September 1972).

"What Is It?" *New Mexico Review* 4, nos. 8–9 (September 1972).

"Whatever Happened to Billy the Kid?" *New Mexico Review* 4, nos. 8–9 (September 1972).

"Trout Fishing in Taos County Streamlets." *Southwest Magazine* 1, no. 1 (September 1972).

"No Comment from Bloom." *New Mexico Review* 4, no. 7 (July 1972).

"A Butterfly Bomb in Taos." *New Mexico Review* 4, no. 6 (June 1972).

"Indian Camp Dam: The Mystery Welded to Reality." *New Mexico Review* 4, nos. 4–5 (April/May 1972).

"Ted Drennan in Taos." *New Mexico Review* 4, no. 3 (March 1972).

"A Man Who Used to Race Horses." *New Mexico Review* 4, no. 2 (February 1972).

"Taos Politics: New Date for Conservancy Hearing."
New Mexico Review 4, no. 2 (February 1972).

"The Plot Thickens in Conservancy Hearings."
New Mexico Review 4, no. 1 (January 1972).

"Taos Politics: Conservancy Hearing Reset for
February 15." *New Mexico Review* 3, no. 12
(December 1971).

"The Miracle is Energy: Aftermath of a Women's
Art Exhibit." *The New Mexico Review* 3, no. 12
(December 1971).

"Reies Lopez Tijerina: A Man Like the Northern
Weather." *New Mexico Review* 3, no. 11 (November
1971).

"The Indian Camp Dam: Requiem for a Way of Life."
New Mexico Review 3, no. 10 (October 1971).

"The Death of Felipe Mares." *New Mexico Review* 3,
nos. 8–9 (August/September 1971).

"Lieutenant William Calley, Meet Kit Carson of Taos."
New Mexico Review 3, nos. 6–7 (June/July 1971).

"A Layman's Impression." *New Mexico Architecture*
13, nos. 5–6 (May/June 1971).

"The People, Yes." *New Mexico Review* 3, no. 5 (May
1971).

"Whatever Happened to Eldorado?" *Motive Magazine*
31, nos. 6–7 (April/May 1971).

"How the Indian Feels." *New Mexico Review* 3, nos. 3–4
(March/April 1971).

"The Blue Lake Blues." *New Mexico Review* 3, no. 1
(January 1971).

"Going to School in Española and Taos." *New Mexico
Review* 2, no. 12 (December 1970).

"Hiroshima Day." *New Mexico Review* 2, no. 11
(November 1970).

"Maria's Encounter with the Police." *New Mexico Review* 2, no. 11 (November 1970).

"Rejecting Fate at Los Alamos." *New Mexico Review* 2, no. 10 (October 1970).

"Human Relations in Taos." *New Mexico Review* 2, nos. 8–9 (August/September 1970).

"Lawrence Martínez—And Don't You Forget Eat." *New Mexico Review* 2, nos. 8–9 (August/September 1970).

"Souvenirs," "Hero," and "Duke." *New Mexico Review* 2, nos. 6–7 (June/July 1970).

"A Man with a Previous Record." *New Mexico Review* 2, no. 5 (May 1970).

"War Is Hell." *Hamilton Spectator* (Hamilton College) (May 13, 1966).

"Anti-Vietnam Riff." *Hamilton Spectator* (Hamilton College) (May 6, 1966).

"After the College Experience." *Hamilton Spectator* (Hamilton College) (April 15, 1966).

"Surreal Nonsense." *Hamilton Spectator* (Hamilton College) (April 8, 1966).

"Homage to Gene Long." *Hamilton Spectator* (Hamilton College) (March 18, 1966).

"Hollywood Babble On." *Hamilton Spectator* (Hamilton College) (March 11, 1966).

"Down in Guatemala." *Hamilton Spectator* (Hamilton College) (March 4, 1966).

"Paco Camino." *Hamilton Spectator* (Hamilton College) (February 18, 1966).

"Guitars: The Reverand Gary Davis." *Hamilton Spectator* (Hamilton College) (May 18, 1962).

"The Hot Corner: Portrait of Tim Gow." *Hamilton Spectator* (Hamilton College) (May 4, 1962).

"A Season of Dying." *The Continental* (Commemorative Edition) (Hamilton College) (1962).

"The Hot Corner: Portrait of Phil Hineline." *Hamilton Spectator* (Hamilton College) (November 10, 1961).

"The Glass Feather." *The Continental* (Commencement Edition) (Hamilton College) (1961).

"The Still, Sad Music." *The Continental* (Hamilton College) (Fall 1960).

"Man." *The Continental* (Hamilton College) (Spring 1960).

"Lagrimas." *The Continental* (Hamilton College) (Fall 1959).

"Noon in Tuscaloosa." *The Loom* (Loomis School) (June 1958).

"On Earth As It Is." *The Loom* (Loomis School) (January 1957).

BOOK INTRODUCTIONS

Quin's Shanghai Circus, by Edward Whittemore. New York: Old Earth Books, 2001.

A Gathering of Wonders, by Joseph Wallace. New York: St. Martin's Press, 2000.

Chokecherries: A S.O.M.O.S Anthology. Vol. 2, edited by Lorraine Ciancio. Taos, N. Mex.: Society of the Muse of the Southwest, 1997.

Generations and Other True Stories, by Bryan Woolley. El Paso: Texas Western Press, 1995.

Enchanted Lifeways: The History, Museums, Arts and Festivals of New Mexico, edited by Ellen Kleiner. Santa Fe, N. Mex.: New Mexico Magazine, 1995.

Explorations, by Ray McSavaney. Los Angeles: Findlay and Sampson Editions, 1992.

Without Discovery: A Native Response to Columbus, edited by Ray González. Seattle: Broken Moon Press, 1992.

The Waning of the West, by Stan Steiner. New York: St. Martin's Press, 1989.

The Art of Rini Templeton, edited by Elizabeth Martínez. Seattle: Real Comet Press, 1988.

The North American Cowboy: A Portrait, by Jay Dusard. Prescott: Consortium Press, 1983.

A Vagabond for Beauty, by Everett Reuss. Salt Lake City: Peregrine Smith, 1983.

The Cowboy from Phantom Banks, by John Brandi. Point Reyes Station, Calif.: Floating Island Publications, 1982.

Seasonal Woman, by Luci Tapahonso. Corrales, N. Mex.: Tooth of Time Books, 1982.

Hablando de Brujas y la Gente de Antes, by Jim Sagel. Austin, Tex.: Place of Herons, 1981.

La Gente de la Luz: Portraits from New Mexico, by Meridel Rubenstein. Santa Fe, N. Mex.: Museum of New Mexico Press, 1977.

ANTHOLOGY APPEARANCES

"A Traffic Violation." In *Getting Over the Color Green: Contemporary Environmental Literature of the Southwest,* edited by Scott Slovic. Tucson: University of Arizona Press, 2001.

"The Enchanted Girl." In *Chokecherries 1999: A S.O.M.O.S. Anthology.* Taos, N. Mex.: S.O.M.O.S., 2000.

"To Make a Long Story Short." In *Francis Ford Coppola's Zoetrope All-Story*, edited by Adrienne Brodeur and Samantha Schnee. New York: Harcourt, 2000.

"Joe Blow and the Llamas." In *Voices from a Sacred Place: In Defense of Petroglyph National Monument*, edited by Verne Huser. Albuquerque: Friends of the Albuquerque Petroglyphs, 1998.

"E=MC². " In *In Pursuit of Happiness: A Left Bank Book*, edited by Linny Stovall. Hillsboro, Oreg.: Blue Heron Publishing, 1995.

"Some Thoughts on Humiliation." In *Discovered Country: Tourism and the American West*, edited by Scott Norris. Albuquerque: Stone Ladder Press, 1994.

"Keep It Simple." In *Being in the World: An Environmental Reader for Writers*, edited by Scott H. Slovic and Terrell F. Dixon. New York: Macmillan, 1993.

"The Day Lee Brodsky Died." In *Sacred Trusts: Essays on Stewardship and Responsibility*, edited by Michael Katakis. San Francisco: Mercury House, 1993.

"Meeting on the Mesa." In *The Endangered Earth: Readings for Writers*, edited by Sarah Morgan and Dennis Okerstrom. Boston: Allyn and Bacon, 1992.

"Keeping It Simple." In *1992 Earth Journal: Environmental Almanac and Resource Directory*, edited by editors of *Buzzworm Magazine*. Boulder: Buzzworm Books, 1992.

"Yo, Thoreau" and "Conscience and Community." In *Heaven Is under Our Feet: A Book for Walden Woods*, edited by Don Henley and Dave Marsh. Stamford, Conn.: Longmeadow Press, 1991.

"The Revolt of Eddie Starner." In *Tierra: Contemporary*

Short Fiction of New Mexico, edited by Rudolfo A. Anaya. El Paso: Cinco Puntos Press, 1989.

Excerpt from *The Milagro Beanfield War.* In *Interior Country: Sories of the Modern West,* edited by Alexander Blackburn, Craig Lesley, and Jill Landem. Athens, Ohio: Swallow Press/Ohio University Press, 1987.

"The Writer As Revolutionary." In *Old Southwest, New Southwest,* edited by Judy Lensink. Tucson: Tucson Public Library, 1987.

"John Nichols." In *Contemporary Authors Autobiography Series.* Vol. 2, edited by Adele Sarkissian. Detroit: Gale Research, 1985.

"Some Words On Behalf of a Predator." In *In Praise of Mountain Lions: Original Praises by Edward Abbey and John Nichols.* Albuquerque: Albuquerque Sierra Club, 1984.

Excerpt from *The Milagro Beanfield War.* In *Writers of the Purple Sage,* edited by Russell Martin and Marc Barasch. New York: Penguin, 1984.

"Death of a Friend." In *Resiembra,* edited by Jim Sagel. Española, N. Mex.: Conjunto Cultural Norteño, 1982.

Exerpt from *The Milagro Beanfield War.* In *Southwest Fiction,* edited by Max Apple. New York: Bantam, 1981.

"Neighbors" and "Politics." In *New America: The Southwest, A Regional View.* Albuquerque: University of New Mexico Press, 1979.

"Newcomers." In *Voices from the Rio Grande: Selections From the First Rio Grande Writers Conference,* edited by Rudolfo Anaya. Albuquerque: Rio Grande Writers Association Press, 1976.

FILM CREDITS

With David Ward. *The Milagro Beanfield War.*
   Produced by Moctesuma Esparza. Directed
   by Robert Redford. Universal Pictures, 1988.
   Screenplay.

The Wizard of Loneliness. Produced by Phil Porcella.
   Directed by Jenny Bowen. Skouras Pictures, 1988.
   Screenplay (uncredited).

Seeds of Survival. Produced and directed by Pamela
   Roberts. National Public Television, 1983.
   Narration.

The Land of Cool Sun. Produced and directed by
   Pamela Roberts. National Public Television,
   1981. Narration.

Missing. Produced by Edward Lewis, Sean Daniels,
   and Guber/Peters. Directed by Costa-Gavras.
   Polygram/Universal, 1981. Screenplay
   (uncredited).

The Sterile Cuckoo. Produced and directed by Alan
   Pakula. Paramount, 1969. Screenplay (uncredited).

SOUND RECORDINGS

Interview by Mike Tilley. KRZA, Alamosa, Colo.,
   January 5, 1999, and December 24, 1998.

"Opening Remarks/Perspectives from New Mexico:
   Charles Wilkinson and John Nichols." Environment 2000, Fourth Annual Conference, Steam-
   boat Springs, Colo., October 16, 1992. Sounds
   True Recordings, Boulder, Colo., 1992.

"Landscapes of a Magic Valley." Readings from *The
   Last Beautiful Days of Autumn* and *On the Mesa.*
   The Audio Press, Inc., Louisville, Colo., 1988.

The Milagro Beanfield War. Read by Cheech Marin. Newman Communications Corporation, Albuquerque, N. Mex., 1986.

Interview by Kay Bonetti. American Audio Prose Library, Albuquerque, N. Mex., April 1982.

Readings from *The Magic Journey* and *The Nirvana Blues.* American Audio Prose Library, Albuquerque, N. Mex., April 1982.

VIDEO RECORDINGS

"Culture, Values, and Money: A Writer Views the North." Lecture. Jim Sagel Memorial Lecture Series: Human Ecology on the Upper Rio Grande, University of New Mexico-Los Alamos, April 6, 1999.

"Growth for the Sake of Growth Is the Ideology of the Cancer Cell." Lecture. Seventh Annual Land Use Conference, Rocky Mountain Land Use Institute, University of Denver College of Law, Denver, Colo., March 12, 1998.

"Milagro Man." Interview. Impact Environmental Reports. News Travel Network, Albuquerque, N. Mex., December 27, 1993.

"A Tribute to Frank Waters." Lecture. Pikes Peak Writers Conference, Colorado Springs, Colo., 1993.

At Week's End. Interview by Roger Morris. KNME, Channel 5, Albuquerque, N. Mex., October 23 and 25, 1992.

"The Sky's the Limit." Documentary on Nichols and his photography. *Colores,* no. 222. Produced and directed by Michael Kamins. KNME, Channel 5, Albuquerque, N. Mex., May 8, 1991.

"High Desert Trout." Fishing interview. *Colores,*
no. 201. Produced and directed by Michael
Kamins. KNME, Channel 5, Albuquerque,
N. Mex., October 10, 1990.

Interview by Hal Rhodes. *On Assignment.* KNME,
Channel 5, Albuquerque, N. Mex., March 9,
1988.

"John Nichols: Magical Realist." Interview by Hal
Rhodes. *The Illustrated Daily,* KNME, Channel 5,
Albuquerque, N. Mex., October 7–8, 1985.

Interview. *Portrait of America: New Mexico.* Directed
by Wayne Ewing. Turner Broadcasting, Atlanta,
Ga., April 9, 1984.

INTERVIEWS

Allen, Steven Robert. "Keeping It Simple: An Interview with John Nichols." *Alibi* 9, no. 25 (June 22,
2000).

Anonymous. "The Universe of John Nichols." *THE
Magazine* (June 1993).

Aydt, Deborah. "An Interview with John Nichols." *El
Palacio* (Museum of New Mexico) 90, no. 2 (July
1984).

Blei, Norbert. "Being in Love with Words and Uncomfortable with Money." *Washington Post*
(March 31, 1985).

Bloom, Lynn Z. "Interview with John Nichols."
Webster Review (Fall 1977).

Bussa, John-Joseph. "Walking a New Mexican Mile."
New Mexico Daily Lobo (October 14, 1992).

Collins, Tom. "Infinity in a Grain of Sand." *Geronimo*
(February 1999).

Collins, Tom. "Myths, Movies, and Mediocrity: Interview with John Nichols." *ARTlines* 3, no. 6 (June 1982).

Cone, Kathy. "On Environmentalism and Environmentalists: An Interview." *Workbook* (Spring 1992).

Conwell, Douglas. "John Nichols' Magic Journey through New Mexico." *Santa Fe New Mexican, Bienvenidos 1985* (1985).

D'Andrea, Patricia. "A Conversation with John Nichols." *La Confluencia* 2, nos. 2–3 (October 1978).

Dunaway, David King. *Writing the Southwest,* edited by David King Dunaway and Sara Spurgeon. New York: Plume, 1995.

Epel, Naomi. *Writers Dreaming,* edited by Naomi Epel. New York: Carol Southern Books, 1993.

Ervin, Ceci. "An Interview with John Nichols." *Crested Butte Chronicle and Pilot* (April 3, 1998).

González, Ray. "Out on a Limb." *Bloomsbury Review* 7, no. 4 (July/August 1987).

González, Ray and John Sullivan. "Armed Visions: John Nichols." In *Living in Words: Interviews from the Bloomsbury Review, 1981–1988,* edited by Gregory McNamee. Portland, Oreg.: Breitenbush Books, 1988.

Harris, Jim. "An Interview with John Nichols." *Greater Llano Estacado Southwest Heritage* 8, no. 3 (Fall 1978).

Jacobsen, Kurt. "An Interview with John Nichols." *Left Curve,* no. 17 (March 1993).

Jongeward, David. "John Nichols: An Interview." *Taos Review,* no. 5 (1992).

Kirk, Amy, Ted Timmer, and Sue Ellinger. "Interview with John Nichols."*Kokopelli's Seed* (Prescott College), no. 5 (Spring 1991).

Kress, Stephen. "The View from Milagro Country." *Crosswinds* 2, no. 6 (August 1990).

Loeffler, Jack. "John Nichols." *Headed Upstream: Interviews with Iconoclasts,* edited by Jack Loeffler. Tucson: Harbinger House, 1989.

March, James. "An Interview with John Nichols '62." *Hamilton Spectator* (Hamilton College) (January 21, 1972).

Marin, Gilbert Varela. "John Nichols, Escritor 'Chicanesco.'" *Revista Rio Bravo* 2, no. 1 (Spring 1982).

Márquez, Tony. "An Interview with John Nichols." *New America* 3, no. 3 (Spring 1979).

McIlvoy, Kevin. "Rudolfo Anaya, John Nichols: A Dialogue." *Puerto Del Sol* 17 (Summer 1982).

Newton, Lisa. "Conversation with John Nichols." *Inkslinger's Review* 2, no.1 (1993).

Ostermann, Robert. "John Nichols: Defying Definition." *Critic* 49, no. 2 (Winter 1994).

Salmon, M. H. "A Conversation with John Nichols." *Basin and Range* 1, no. 3 (September/October 1985).

Schulman, Heidi. "Resumé: John Nichols Interview." *New Mexico Business Journal* 2, no. 10 (November 1978).

Scmidt, Dorey, and Adelle Mery. "Interview with John Nichols." *Texas College English* (Fall 1991).

Skenazy, Paul. "An Interview with John Nichols." *In These Times* (December 9, 1981). Reprinted in *San Francisco Review of Books* (June 1982).

Stack, Allyson. "Art and Political Action: An Interview with John Nichols." *Alligator Juniper* (Prescott College), no. 6 (2000).

Stucky, David. "Profile: John Nichols." *Conceptions Southwest* (Spring 1985).

Sullivan, John. "The Scribe of Taos." *Bloomsbury Review* 1, no. 6 (September/October 1981).

Thompson, Phyllis. *This Is about Vision: Interviews with Southwestern Writers,* edited by John F. Crawford, William Balassi, and Annie O. Eysturoy. Albuquerque: University of New Mexico Press, 1990.

VanderPlas, Jaap. "Every Stone You Throw Has Ripples Out Infinitely." *ARTlines* (Winter 1986/87).

Welch, Bryan. "John Nichols Doesn't Go Hollywood." *Taos News* (January 3, 1985).

BIOGRAPHICAL/CRITICAL STUDIES AND BOOK REVIEWS

Abas, Bryan. "Coors Doesn't Sell in Milagro." *Westword* (March 30, 1988).

Ahlstrom, Tim and Bob Skippon. Review of "Lagrimas" (uncollected short story). *Hamilton Spectator* (Hamilton College) (January 8, 1960).

Alford, Steven. "Flashbacks to Vietnam." Review of *American Blood. Fort Lauderdale News/Sun Sentinel* (May 31, 1987).

Anderson, Elliott. "An Epic Tale of Cultural Genocide in the Name of Progress." Review of *The Magic Journey. Chicago Tribune* (April 9, 1978).

Anderson, Terry. "John Nichols: Writer's Writer—in the Purest Sense of Term." *Denver Post Book World* (May 14, 1978).

Ashton, John. "Author Talks about His Life, Success, Books." *Rocky Mountain News,* Lifestyles section (August 7, 1981).

Backes, Clarus. "Author Doesn't Act Like a Big Fish." *Denver Post* (December 14, 1982).

Bannon, Barbara. Review of *The Nirvana Blues. Publishers Weekly* 219, no. 24 (June 12, 1981).

Barbato, Joseph. "A Wild, Macho Mix-up of a Man." Review of *A Ghost in the Music. Newsday* (November 25, 1979).

Barber, Joe. "New Nichols Narrative Richly Hued Treasure." Review of *If Mountains Die. Colorado Springs Gazette-Telegraph* (February 23, 1980).

Barkham, John. "Two Authors Vary Styles." *New York World Telegram and Sun* (January 15, 1965).

Beasley, Conger, Jr. *"Mesa* Celebrates Southwest." Review of *On the Mesa. Kansas City Star* (June 22, 1986).

Beaven, Scott. "New Mexico Novel Reaps High Praise." Review of *The Milagro Beanfield War. Albuquerque Journal* (October 13, 1974).

Becker, Alida. "Assault and Battery by Way of Vietnam." Review of *American Blood. Newsday* (May 6, 1987).

Benke, Richard. "Author John Nichols Doubles Workload." *Chieftain* (September 21, 1997). Reprinted in *Santa Fe New Mexican* (September 28, 1997).

Bernikow, Louise. Review of *An Elegy for September. Cosmopolitan* (June 1992).

Best, Allen. "Living on $5,000/Yr." *Vail Trail* (November 2, 1990).

Black, Charlotte. "John Nichols Leaves Taos for

'Quiet' of Albuquerque." *Albuquerque Tribune*
(January 16, 1984).

———. "Experience Goes a Long Way for Nichols."
Albuquerque Tribune (July 22, 1977).

Blaustein, Arthur I. "Progress and Poverty—Sunbelt
Style." Review of *The Magic Journey. National
Economic Development and Law Center Report*
(September/October 1979).

Blei, Norbert. "John Nichols' Novel Is a Poem to
New Mexico." Review of *An Elegy for September.
Minneapolis Star Tribune* (November 8, 1992).

———. "A Man for One Season—Autumn." Review
of *The Last Beautiful Days of Autumn. Milwaukee
Journal* (September 26, 1982).

Blessing, Dick. "For Pookie, with Love and Good
Riddance: John Nichols' *The Sterile Cuckoo."*
Review of *The Sterile Cuckoo. Journal of Popular
Culture* 7 (1973).

———. Review of "Peace and a Soul" (uncollected
poem). *Hamilton Spectator* (Hamilton College)
(April 7, 1961).

Bloom, Lynn Z. "A Comic, Ironic Trilogy Ends in
Tattered Dreams." Review of *The Nirvana Blues.
Cleveland Plain Dealer* (August 2, 1981).

Bonilla, Carlos. "New Mexico Trilogy Author Believes
Everyone Is Political." *La Mecha* (December 9,
1986).

Bowden, Charles. "Not Just Another Pastel Coyote."
Review of *An Elegy for September. Los Angeles Times*
(June 28, 1992).

Bowman, Jon. "John Nichols: Taos Author Savors
Life on the Edge." *New Mexico Magazine* (January
1988).

Boyd, Gordon. "Nichols Always Fighting Battle: Between Writing and Action, Ya Know." *Utica Daily Press* (October 10, 1968).

Bromley, Larry. "A Dazzlement of Surprise." Review of *The Last Beautiful Days of Autumn. Dallas Morning News* (January 2, 1983).

Brown, Paul. "A Literary View of the Southwest: Seven Authors in the Land That Inspired Them." *Dallas Morning News, Dallas Life Magazine* (October 18, 1987).

Bruce-Novoa, Juan. "Década Literaria Chicana." *La Opinión,* no. 128 (January 2, 1983).

Buchholtz, C. W. Review of *On the Mesa. Rocky Mountain News* (November 2, 1986).

Bulow, Ernie. "Taos Country Hymn." Review of *A Fragile Beauty. Gallup Independent* (January 2, 1988).

Burnside, Gordon. "Western Black Humor." Review of *The Nirvana Blues. St. Louis Magazine* (October 1981).

Busch, Frederick. Review of *The Milagro Beanfield War. New York Times Book Review* (October 27, 1974).

Carlin, Margaret. "Rage in His Writing: John Nichols Puts Ideology on Paper." *Rocky Mountain News* (May 24, 1987).

Carlson, Ron. "Love in the Trenches." Review of *Conjugal Bliss. Los Angeles Times Book Review* (April 24, 1994).

Carroll, Mary. Review of *Conjugal Bliss. Booklist* 90, no. 9 (January 12, 1994).

Casey, Constance. "Brutal Vision of Post-Vietnam America." Review of *American Blood. San José Mercury News* (May 10, 1987).

Chanin, Abe. "A Bittersweet Social Commentary."

Review of *The Milagro Beanfield War*. *Arizona Daily Star* (October 27, 1974).

Clark, Tom. "Scary Skeleton of Vietnam: Veteran's Psychological Turmoil Is a Brutal Tale." Review of *American Blood*. *Denver Post* (May 3, 1987).

Clark, William. "John Nichols: 'A Fervent Belief in the Power of Art to Create Change' Motivates His Work." *Publishers Weekly* 241, no. 7 (February 14, 1994).

Clinch, Minty. "When Polemicist Meets Superstar." *London (England) Independent* (August 17, 1988).

Clifford, Susan. Review of *Conjugal Bliss*. *Library Journal* 119, no. 1 (January 1994).

Colby, Vineta. "Nichols, John (Treadwell)." *World Authors, 1980–1985*, edited by Vineta Colby. New York: H. W. Wilson Company, 1991.

Conaway, Ed. "A Rocky Mountain Trip between Reality and Fantasy." Review of *The Nirvana Blues*. *San Francisco Chronicle* (August 23, 1981).

Connelly, Christopher. "The Milagro Muddle." *Premiere Magazine* (March 1988).

Cook, Bruce. "A Half-Baked Miracle Awakens a Sleepy Town." Review of *The Magic Journey*. *Washington Post Book World* (June 17, 1978).

Creighton, Jim. "Facing Up to a Life's September." Review of *An Elegy for September*. *St. Louis Post-Dispatch* (June 14, 1992).

Cromie, Robert A. "A Lucky Twenty-Three Year Old." *Chicago Tribune* (March 1964). Reprinted in *Hamilton Alumni Review* (Summer 1964).

Crowder, Joan. "Nichols Strips *American Blood* from the Pages." *Santa Barbara News-Press* (May 22, 1987).

Crowdus, Gary. "The Missing Dossier: An Interview with Costa-Gavras." *Cineaste* 12, no. 1 (1982).

———. "A Review of *Missing.*" *Cineaste* 12, no. 1 (1982).

Cryer, Dan. "Wed for Better (Sex), Lots Worse (Combat)." Review of *Conjugal Bliss. Newsday* (February 7, 1994).

Curley, Thomas. "The Growing Pains of Pookie Adams." Review of *The Sterile Cuckoo. New York Times Book Review* (January 17, 1965).

D'Andrea, Patricia. Review of *The Magic Journey. La Confluencia* 2, no. 4 (1978).

Delbanco, Nicholas. "Two Doomed Passions." Review of *An Elegy for September. Chicago Tribune* (July 5, 1992).

DeLuca, Vincent. Review of "The Still, Sad Music" (uncollected short story). *Hamilton Spectator* (Hamilton College) (December 9, 1960).

Dewees, Charles L. "Nichols Scores with *Beanfield.*" Review of *The Milagro Beanfield War. Mobile Press Register* (May 18, 1975).

Dire, Angela. "Author John Nichols Turns Talents to Vietnam." *Colorado Springs Gazette Telegraph* (February 7, 1987).

Dold, Gaylord. "Skilled Writer Misses the Mark." Review of *An Elegy for September. Wichita Eagle* (August 16, 1992).

Drabanski, Emily. "Southwest Bookshelf: *On the Mesa.*" Review of *On the Mesa. New Mexico Magazine* (December 1986).

Dretzka, Gary. ". . . and a Novel in Kind." Review of *A Ghost in the Music. Los Angeles Herald Examiner* (September 23, 1979).

Duman, Dick. "Artistic Visions of the Present and Past." Review of *A Fragile Beauty. Bloomsbury Review* 8, no. 4 (July/August 1988).

Dunn, J. A. C. "A Smoldering Anger." Review of *American Blood. St. Petersburg Times* (June 21, 1987).

Dutton, Dennis H. Review of *Keep It Simple. New Mexico Magazine* (June 1993).

Dykhuis, Randy. Review of *The Sky's the Limit. Library Journal* 115, no. 13 (August 1990).

———. Review of *On the Mesa. Library Journal* 111, no. 12 (July 16, 1986).

Eastburn, Kathryn. "John Nichols' Blissful Blues: Thoughts on the Planet, Relationships, and the Survival of the Species." *Colorado Springs Independent* (April 6, 1994).

Eder, Richard. "Vietnam: Uncured Plague of Violence in America." Review of *American Blood. Los Angeles Times Book Review* (April 29, 1987).

Edwards, Page. Review of *The Last Beautiful Days of Autumn. Library Journal* 107, no. 19 (November 1, 1982).

———. Review of *The Nirvana Blues. Library Journal* 106, no. 10 (May 15, 1981).

Ellis, Reuben J. "Fast Breaking Story! Paranoia and Self-Consciousness in John Nichols' Use of Mock Headlines." *Southwestern American Literature* 13, no. 1 (Fall 1987).

Engley, Hollis L. "A Book of Beauty, but with a Risk." Review of *A Fragile Beauty. Santa Fe New Mexican* (March 19, 1988).

Evans, Clay. "Nichols Escapes Beanfield for the Politics of Marriage." *Boulder Sunday Camera* (March 6, 1994).

Fallon, D'Arcy. "Cupid's Curmudgeon." *Colorado Springs Gazette Telegraph* (April 18, 1994).

Fanning, Garth. "Brilliant Novel Tells of Boy's Search for Reason for Living." Review of *The Wizard of Loneliness. Sacramento Bee* (March 13, 1966).

Ferguson, Linda W. "Displacing a Culture." Review of *The Nirvana Blues. Bloomsbury Review* 1, no. 6 (September/October 1981).

Fibich, Linda. "A Rhapsody on the Healing Powers of the Earth." Review of *On the Mesa. Dallas Times Herald* and *Salt Lake Deseret News* (June 7, 1986).

Fisher, Barbara. Review of *An Elegy for September. New York Times Book Review* (June 21, 1992).

Flaum, Dave. "Born Losers All." Review of *The Milagro Beanfield War. Hartford Courant* (October 27, 1974).

Fleming, Thomas J. "The Sorrows of Wendall." Review of *The Wizard of Loneliness. New York Times Book Review* (March 6, 1966).

Forman, Joanne. "Nichols Recommends Keeping It Simple." *Taos News* (October 30, 1997).

———. "John Nichols' *The Sky's the Limit.*" *Taos Magazine* (November/December 1990).

Foss, Phillip. "Thank God Nature Can Still Kick Me in the Teeth!" *Santa Fe Reporter, Voices* (Summer 1979).

Fremont-Smith, Eliot. "Life with Pookie, Life Without." Review of *The Sterile Cuckoo. New York Times* (January 15, 1965).

Friedman, Max J. "Modern Greek Drama On a Movie Location." Review of *A Ghost in the Music. Chicago Tribune Book World* (October 7, 1979).

Gallagher, Hugh. "Nichols' New Novel: Important Statement on New Mexico." Review of *The Magic Journey. Albuquerque Journal* (April 16, 1978).

Gaughan, Thomas. Review of *An Elegy for September.* *Booklist* 88, no. 17 (May 1, 1992).

Getz, Bob. "Not So 'BLISS'ful: Marriage Gives License to Argue." *Fort Collins Coloradoan* (March 6, 1994).

Girth, Glenn. "John Nichols' Comedy Eases the Pain." Review of *Conjugal Bliss. Denver Post* (March 6, 1994).

Grabinger, R. Scott. Review of *A Fragile Beauty. Colorado Libraries* (June 1988).

Graham, Jennifer W. "Rising Stars: John Nichols." *Horizon Magazine* 25, no. 3 (April 1982).

Graham, Olive. "John Nichols Chronicles Me-Generation Malaise." Review of *The Nirvana Blues. Austin Chronicle* (October 16, 1981).

Greenwood, Phaedra. "An Avalanche of Words: John Nichols Looks Back at a Lifetime of Writing." *Taos News, Tempo* (February 24, 2000).

———. "John Nichols Remembers the Road to Milagro." *Taos News, Tempo* (April 16, 1998).

Gregg, Louise. "Grandeur of New Mexico Forges People's Character." Review of *A Fragile Beauty. Wichita Falls Times Record News* (February 27, 1988).

Greth, Carlos Vidal. "Savagery and Stereotypes." Review of *American Blood. Austin American-Statesman* (June 14, 1987).

"Grey Hair, Rejections Not Nichols' Bag." *Taos News* (December 4, 1969).

Groves, Bob. "John Nichols Raging, and the National Soul." Review of *American Blood. Albuquerque Journal, Impact Magazine* (April 28, 1987).

Grumbach, Doris. Review of *If Mountains Die. New York Times Book Review* (June 10, 1979).

Grutzmacher, Harold M. Review of *The Sterile Cuckoo. Chicago Tribune* (January 17, 1965).

Guy, David. "After 'Nam: A Savage, Exaggerated Critique of American Life." Review of *American Blood. Chicago Tribune* (April 19, 1987).

Haederle, Michael. "The 'Beanfield' Burden." *Los Angeles Times* (April 20, 1994).

Hall, Barbara Hodge. " 'Self' Search in the Wild." Review of *On the Mesa. Anniston (Ala.) Star* (August 10, 1986).

Hall, Rosanna. "Taos Author Captures Drama of Small Farmers." *Santa Fe New Mexican* (July 8, 1979).

———. "Nichols' New Book on Taos Captivating." Review of *If Mountains Die. Santa Fe New Mexican* (June 10, 1979).

Hallgren, Sherri. "The World on a Fling." Review of *An Elegy for September. San Francisco Chronicle* (September 6, 1992).

Halloran, Kathleen. "In Self Defense: To Save His Own Life, Author Fights to Save Ours." *Fort Collins Coloradoan* (October 26, 1990).

Hanley, Mark. "A Haunted September Song." Review of *An Elegy for September. Staten Island Advance* (July 19, 1992).

Hanson, Susan. "Nichols Describes Writing Profession As Hard Work." *San Marcos (Tex.) Daily Record* (October 14, 1994).

Heggen, Russ. "A Man in Love . . . with the Land and with Words." Review of *Landscapes of a Magic*

Valley. Travelin': Exploring the Backroads and Byways of the West 2, no. 3 (May/June 1991).

Hemesath, James. Review of *American Blood. Library Journal* 112, no. 7 (April 15, 1987).

Henderson, David W. Review of *An Elegy for September. Library Journal* 117, no. 10 (June 1, 1992).

Hendrix, Sharon. "Taos Author John Nichols Sees Role of Writer As Social Critic." *Hobbs Daily News-Sun* (November 2, 1986).

Hepworth, James R. Review of *Dancing on the Stones. Bloomsbury Review* 20, no. 3 (May/June 2000).

Heredia, Rick. "Nichols Captures Essence of New Mexico's Beauty." Review of *A Fragile Beauty. Colorado Springs Gazette Telegraph* (April 3, 1988).

Hicks, Granville. Review of *The Wizard of Loneliness. Saturday Review* (February 26, 1966).

Hill, Pamyla. "Exploitation, Injustice Recurrent Themes in Nichols' Work . . ." *Alamosa (Colo.) Valley Courier* (July 17, 1991).

———. "Nichols Politics Like Brown, Asimov, Carson, Muir." *Alamosa (Colo.) Valley Courier* (July 17, 1991).

———. "Writing Now a Career for NY-to-Taos Transplant." *Alamosa (Colo.) Valley Courier* (July 17, 1991).

Hirsch, Kathleen. "A Viet Vet's Unceasing Battle." Review of *American Blood. Washington Post Book World* (May 11, 1987).

Hood, Ann. "The Thirty-Day Romance." Review of *An Elegy for September. Washington Post Book World* (July 17, 1992).

Howard, Alan. "The Hot Corner: Portrait of John

Nichols." *Hamilton Spectator* (Hamilton College) (May 18, 1962).

Howell, Leon. "One Lousy Beanfield." *Christianity and Crisis* 48, no. 9 (June 6, 1988).

Huff, Alice. Review of *The Sky's the Limit. PSA Journal* 59, no. 7 (July 1993).

Jacobsen, Janet L. "Study Guide for *The Milagro Beanfield War* by John T. Nichols." Angle of Vision Project. Tempe: Arizona State University, 1986.

"John Nichols: Beanfield War Battled Close to Home." *Taos News* (September 26, 1974).

"John Nichols' *The Sterile Cuckoo*." Review of *The Sterile Cuckoo. New Yorker* (March 1965).

Johnson, Diane. "The War Between the Sexes." Review of *Conjugal Bliss. Vogue* (February 1994).

Johnson, Lucy. "Seeking a Lost Childhood, a Boy Finds a New World." Review of *The Wizard of Loneliness. Milwaukee Journal* (February 27, 1966).

Jones, Caroly. "Novelist Finds Fulfillment in New Mexico Community." *Albuquerque Journal* (July 5, 1981).

Kane, George. "Beanfield Parable Deeply Rooted in Humanism." Review of *The Milagro Beanfield War. Rocky Mountain News* (April 13, 1975).

Katel, Peter. "Singer of the Nirvana Blues." *Scottsdale Progress, Saturday Magazine* (October 3, 1981).

Kearny, Jill. "The Old Gringo." *American Film* 13, no. 5 (March 1988).

Kendig, Tamara. "Dreaming of Home: Magic Realism in William Faulkner, Gabriel Garcia Márquez, Toni Morrison, and John Nichols." *Dissertation Abstracts International* (May 8, 1998).

Kenny, Ed. Review of "A Season of Dying" (uncollected short story). *Hamilton Spectator* (Hamilton College) (May 18, 1962).

Kisling, Jack. "A Man's Vision: John Nichols Finds Some Time Amid Writing to Espouse Causes." *Denver Post* (April 20, 1986).

———. "Chill Tone of Nichols' *Nirvana* Distresses." *Denver Post* (August 16, 1981).

———. "Taos Valley Would Seem to Be Right Place." Review of *If Mountains Die. Denver Post* (June 10, 1979).

———. "*Magic Journey:* Ghosts for All." *Denver Post* (May 21, 1978).

Krauzer, Steven M. *"Blues* by John Nichols." *Rocky Mountain Magazine* (September 1981).

Krim, Seymour. Review of *If Mountains Die. Village Voice* (September 30, 1979).

Kunk, Deborah. "'Milagro' Country: In John Nichols' Landscapes All Things Seem Possible." *Los Angeles Herald Examiner* (March 18, 1988).

Lenderman, Andy. "A Maverick's Journey." *Albuquerque Tribune* (August 25, 2000).

Levin, Martin. Review of *A Ghost in the Music. New York Times Book Review* (October 28, 1979).

Lewis, Robert. Review of *A Fragile Beauty. North Dakota Quarterly* (Summer 1988).

Liberatore, Karen. "The Bee Lady and the Mesa Man." Review of *On the Mesa. San Francisco Chronicle* (June 8, 1986).

Litke, James. "Unholy Place." Review of *The Milagro Beanfield War. New Haven Register* (October 13, 1974).

Loftis, J. E. "Community As Protagonist in *The Milagro Beanfield War*." *Rocky Mountain Review of Language and Literature* (Winter 1984).

López, Antonio. "Essays of an Adopted Son." Review of *Dancing on the Stones. Santa Fe New Mexican* (May 14, 2000).

López, Ruth. "Book Notes: John Nichols." *Santa Fe New Mexican* (February 6, 2000).

Lottman, Eileen. Review of *The Milagro Beanfield War. Harper's Bookletter* (January 6, 1975).

Lucia, Ellis. *"If Mountains Die* Old Story." *Portland Oregonian* (August 26, 1979).

Lynch, Donna. "Novel Is Haunting, Beautiful." Review of *The Wizard of Loneliness. Baton Rouge Sunday Advocate* (October 9, 1966).

MacNaughton, Anne. "Nichols Defends the Earth with Pictures." Review of *The Sky's the Limit. Taos News, Tempo* (October 11, 1990).

MacNeil, William A. "Life's Journey So Far Pleases 'Milagro' Writer Nichols." *Albuquerque Journal* (December 22, 1996).

Magness, Perre. *"Conjugal Bliss* Boils Down to Dull Goulash." *Memphis Commercial Appeal* (February 20, 1994).

Mahood, Jan. "Deft Touch of Young Author Spells Genuine Depth of Character in Novel." Review of *The Wizard of Loneliness. Hartford Times* (February 26, 1966).

Malone, Paul Scott. "Lolita's Legacy: A Girl, a Writer and a Doomed Love Affair." Review of *An Elegy for September. Dallas Morning News* (August 16, 1992).

Markmann, Charles Lam. "Joe and the Beanstalk."

Review of *The Milagro Beanfield War*. *Los Angeles Times Book Review* (November 24, 1974).

Márquez, Antonio. "The Promise and Failure of Literatura Chicanesca." *New Mexico Humanities Review* 4, no. 1 (Spring 1981).

Martin, Russell. "Writers of the Purple Sage." *New York Times Magazine* (December 27, 1981).

Martínez, Demetria. "Food for Thought: From Beanfield Wars to Mushrooms, Author John Nichols Offers a Delightful Mouthful of Global Reflection." *Tucson Weekly* (October 9, 1997).

Martínez, Guadalupe. Review of *On the Mesa*. *Albuquerque Journal, Impact Magazine* (April 29, 1986).

McCarthy, John. "Gentle Film Bucks a Violent Society." *Lewiston (Idaho) Morning Tribune* (April 27, 1988).

McCollum, Malcolm. "John Nichols: A Small Celebration of His Work." Colorado Springs: Great Big Elephant Press, 1996 (limited edition pamphlet).

McLellan, Joseph. "Trouble in Paradise." Review of *The Nirvana Blues*. *Washington Post Book World* (August 28, 1981).

McManus, Patricia. "A Bird in Hand." Review of *The Sterile Cuckoo*. *New York Herald Tribune Book Week* (January 24, 1965).

Meighan, Patrick. "'The Sky's the Limit' for *Milagro* Author Nichols." *Greeley (Colo.) Tribune* (October 28, 1990).

Mentzinger, Bob. *"Keep It Simple:* Nichols' New Collection of Minimalist Photos." *Taos News* (December 17, 1992).

Mergendahl, Peter. "Author's New Tactic Shocking." Review of *American Blood*. *Rocky Mountain News* (May 24, 1987).

Miller, Tom. "The Embattled Beanfield." *Phoenix New Times* (November 19, 1986). Reprinted in *Tuscon Weekly* (December 17, 1986).

Milligan, Bryce. "Welcome to a 'Marriage from Hell.'" Review of *Conjugal Bliss*. *Chicago Tribune* (February 27, 1994).

Mills, Stephen. Review of *The Sky's the Limit*. *Times Literary Supplement* (September 13, 1991).

Mondin, Sandra. "The Depiction of the Chicana in *Bless Me, Ultima* and *The Milagro Beanfield War: A Study in Contrasts*." In *Mexico and the United States: Intercultural Relations in the Humanities*, edited by Juanita Luna Lawhn, Juan Bruce-Novoa, Guillermo Campos, and Ramón Saldívar. San Antonio, Tex.: San Antonio College, 1984.

Montelibre, María. "Puntos de vista de un afamado escritor." *Tiempo Latino* (July 5, 1989).

Moore, Andrew O. Review of *On the Mesa*. *Environmental Action* (September/October 1986).

Moore, Jack D. "A Failing Competitor." Review of *The Wizard of Loneliness*. *Tampa Tribune* (April 10, 1966).

Moore, John. "Author Opposes Water Districts." *Durango Herald* (April 1, 1979).

Mungo, Ray. "Terrible Price of War." Review of *American Blood*. *San Francisco Examiner-Chronicle* (April 19, 1987).

Murray, John A. "Northern New Mexico: The Milagro Beanfield War," and "John Nichols." In *Cinema Southwest: An Illustrated Guide to the Movies and*

Their Locations. Flagstaff, Ariz.: Northland Publishing, 2000.

Nabhan, Gary. Review of *If Mountains Die. High Country News* (September 21, 1979).

Nathan, Jean. "Andrés Martínez and the Beanfield: A Cañon Man and His Friends Gave John Nichols a Novel." *Albuquerque Journal, Impact Magazine* (October 28, 1986).

Nathan, Jean. "John Nichols: Writer, Philosopher, Idealist and Shed Builder." *Taos News, Tempo* (April 23, 1987).

Niederman, Sharon. "John Nichols Spills the Beans." *Santa Fe Reporter* (March 4, 1992).

———. "Nichols in Hollywood: The Movie Version." *Santa Fe Reporter* (March 4, 1992).

Nizalowski, John. "Elegizing Lost Youth . . ." Review of *An Elegy for September. Ridgway (Colo.) Sun* (January 7, 1993).

Nobles, Mike. "Stock Pond Becomes Heroine in *On the Mesa." Western Colorado Congress Clarion* (July 1998).

Nolan, Tom. "Entering John Nichols' Blue Heaven." Review of *The Nirvana Blues. Los Angeles Herald Examiner* (August 23, 1981).

"'Oh My God, What's This?' Literary Tree Ranking with Post-Its." *Esquire* 112, no. 1 (July 1989).

O'Neill, John. "A Very Funny Novel If . . . Ugh!" Review of *The Wizard of Loneliness. Atlanta Journal and Constitution* (March 6, 1966).

Orme, Terry. "John Nichols, Star of Page and Screen." *Salt Lake Tribune* (June 8, 1986).

———. "Shades of *Walden* on a Desert Mesa." Review of *On the Mesa. Salt Lake Tribune* (June 8, 1986).

Otis, John W. "Hear a Ghost in the Music?" Review of *A Ghost in the Music*. *Minneapolis Tribune* (November 25, 1979).

Pellow, C. Kenneth. "John Nichols, Regionalist and Reformer." *Writers Forum* 12 (Fall 1986).

———. "The Transformation of *The Sterile Cuckoo*." *Literature/Film Quarterly* 5 (1977).

Petersen, David. "The Milagro Man." *Denver Post, Empire Magazine* (November 2, 1997).

———. "*Keep It Simple* Is Nichols' Personal Defense of the Earth." *Durango Herald* (March 4, 1993).

———. "All That's Worth Saving." Review of *The Sky's the Limit*. *Bloomsbury Review* 11, no. 3 (April/May 1991).

Pfeil, Fred. "Down the Beanstalk." Review of *American Blood, The Magic Journey, The Milagro Beanfield War,* and *The Nirvana Blues*. *The Nation* 244, no. 24 (June 20, 1987).

Pinsker, Sanford. "John Nichols' Postage Stamp of Southwestern Culture." *New America* 4, no. 2 (Summer 1980).

Pintarich, Paul. "A Postwar Horror Story." Review of *American Blood*. *Portland Oregonian* (June 7, 1987).

Polk, Tony. "A Chronicler of Contemporary Struggles." *Rocky Mountain News* (Summer 1977).

Porter, Bruce. "Small Boy on His Own." Review of *The Wizard of Loneliness*. *Providence Journal* (April 10, 1966).

"Portraits of Distinguished Theta Delts: John Nichols, Psi '42: Beyond the *Sterile Cuckoo*." *Shield of Theta Delta Chi* (Spring/Summer 1982).

Prose, Francine. "Fiction in Review." Review of *Conjugal Bliss*. *Yale Review* (1994).

Prufer, Mona. "The Fragile Beauty of the Milagro Country." Review of *A Fragile Beauty*. *Alternatives Magazine* (February 19, 1988).

Pryce-Jones, Alan. "Ambitious, Weak Novel, but . . ." Review of *The Wizard of Loneliness*. *New York Herald Tribune* (February 24, 1966).

Purdy, John C. "Visions of John Nichols." *Ghost Ranch Journal* 1, no. 1 (Winter 1986).

Querry, Ron. "Nichols: Costilla Seed for Milagro." *Taos News* (June 12, 1986).

Ramsey, Ron. "John Nichols Weaves Poignant Story about the Passages of Life." Review of *An Elegy for September*. *Santa Fe New Mexican, Pasatiempo* (August 7, 1992).

Read, David W. "When Words and Emotions Are Merged." Review of *The Wizard of Loneliness*. *St. Louis Post-Dispatch* (March 20, 1966).

Rennert, Maggie. Review of *The Wizard of Loneliness*. *New York Herald Tribune Book Week* (February 20, 1966).

Review of *A Fragile Beauty*. *Outside* (March 1988).

Review of *A Ghost in the Music*. *New York Times Book Review* (October 28, 1979).

Review of *American Blood*. *Kirkus Reviews* (March 1, 1987).

Review of *An Elegy for September*. *Kirkus Reviews* (April 15, 1992).

Review of *Conjugal Bliss*. *Publishers Weekly* 240, no. 50 (December 13, 1993).

Review of *Landscapes of a Magic Valley*. *Publishers Weekly* 234, no. 15 (October 7, 1988).

Review of *On the Mesa*. *Westways* (September 1986).

Review of *On the Mesa*. *Publishers Weekly* 229, no. 16 (April 18, 1986).

Review of *The Last Beautiful Days of Autumn*. *Library Journal* 107, no. 19 (November 1, 1982).

Review of *The Magic Journey*. *New York Times Book Review* (April 16, 1978).

Review of *The Nirvana Blues*. *Publishers Weekly* 223, no. 11 (March 18, 1983).

Ribera-Ortega, Pedro. "Una Hermosura Frágil." Review of *A Fragile Beauty*. *Santa Fe Reporter* (March 30, 1988).

Robertson, Don. "When You're Eleven the World Is an Enemy." Review of *The Wizard of Loneliness*. *Cleveland Plain Dealer* (April 10, 1966).

Rowen, James. "A Memoir in Splendor." Review of *If Mountains Die*. *Los Angeles Herald Examiner* (September 23, 1979).

Rubel, David. "John Nichols." *The Reading List: Contemporary Fiction: A Critical Guide to the Complete Works of 110 Authors,* edited by David Rubel. New York: Henry Holt Owl Books, 1998.

Rumley, Larry. "Wild and Wonderful." Review of *The Milagro Beanfield War*. *Seattle Times* (November 24, 1974).

Russell, Inez. "John Nichols Enters the Land of Confusion." *Albuquerque Tribune* (June 9, 1992).

Samson, Sue. Review of *Dancing on the Stones*. *Library Journal* 125, no. 2 (February 1, 2000).

Sánchez, Arley. "There Is a Season . . . : Author Comes of Age in 'An Elegy for September.'" Review of *An Elegy for September*. *Albuquerque Journal* (July 24, 1992).

Sapolin, Donna. "No Man Is an Oasis Here." *Metropolitan Home* 20, no. 9 (September 1988).

Saunders, Rebecca. "Nichols Makes Earthy Point at Lit Conference." *Now Magazine* (October 4, 1990).

Schneider, Wolf. "Words on the Wind: The Spirit of the West Lives On." *Santa Fe New Mexican, Pasatiempo* (November 6, 1982).

Scott, Jay. "A Southwestern War and Peace." Review of *The Magic Journey. Toronto Globe and Mail* (April 29, 1978).

See, Carolyn. Review of *The Last Beautiful Days of Autumn. Los Angeles Times Book Review* (August 26, 1982).

———. "The Wilderness Life, with All Those Squishy Details." *Los Angeles Times Book Review.* (August 26, 1982).

———. "Drives and Dreams and Adobes." Review of *The Nirvana Blues. Los Angeles Times Book Review* (August 16, 1981).

Seghers, Frances. "Ethnic Plight Turned into Unique Story." Review of *The Milagro Beanfield War. Baton Rouge Sunday Advocate* (December 8, 1974).

Shirley, Carl. "John Nichols." *Dictionary of Literary Biography: Yearbook 1982,* edited by Richard Ziegfeld. Detroit: Gale Research, 1983.

Simpson, Sherry. "The Writer's Life Knows No Limits." Review of *Dancing on the Stones. San Francisco Chronicle Book Review* (July 9, 2000).

Skenazy, Paul. "A Long, Long Way from Nirvana." Review of *The Nirvana Blues. In These Times* (December 9, 1981).

Slattery, Robert. "John Nichols: His Blood and Guts." *Route Sixty Six* (September 1987).

Slovic, Scott. "Be Prepared for the Worst: Love, Anticipated Loss, and Environmental Valuation." *Western American Literature* (Fall 2000).

Smith, Wendy. "Bride and Gloom." Review of *Conjugal Bliss*. *New York Times Book Review* (March 13, 1994).

Smyth, Russell. "Nichols Plots Western Land Use Wars." *Montrose (Colo.) Daily Press* (October 26, 1998).

Sobczak, A. J. Review of *Conjugal Bliss*. Magill Book Reviews for Dow Jones News/Retrieval: Salem Press, Inc. (1994).

Sonnichsen, C. L. Review of *The Nirvana Blues*. *El Paso Herald-Post* (October 16, 1981).

St. Charnez, Casey. "At Last: *The Milagro Beanfield War*—Here's Your Quick Guide to the Movie, and More." *Santa Fe Reporter* (March 16, 1988).

St. Pierre, Brian. "Irony after the Altar." Review of *Conjugal Bliss*. *San Francisco Chronicle* (February 20, 1994).

Steinberg, Sybil. Review of *Conjugal Bliss*. *Publishers Weekly* 240, no. 50 (December 13, 1993).

———. Review of *An Elegy for September*. *Publishers Weekly* 239, no. 19 (April 20, 1992).

———. Review of *American Blood*. *Publishers Weekly* 231, no. 9 (March 6, 1987).

Stuttaford, Genevieve. Review of *On the Mesa*. *Publishers Weekly* 229, no. 16 (April 18, 1986).

Sullivan, John. Review of *If Mountains Die*. *Smithsonian* 10, no. 4 (July 1979).

Swerdlow, Joel. "Love That Makes Loved Ones Suffer." Review of *A Ghost in the Music. Detroit News* (September 23, 1979).

Tatum, Stephen L. "Nichols Warbles Variations on a Theme by Thoreau." Review of *On the Mesa. Fort Worth Star-Telegram* (November 16, 1986).

Taylor, Mark. "Nichols' 'Mesa' Mixes Lore, Louts and Love." Review of *On the Mesa. Albuquerque Tribune* (May 14, 1986).

Terry, Marshall. "Ai Chihuahua! A Rare Writer." Review of *The Milagro Beanfield War. Dallas Morning News* (January 12, 1975).

Thomas, J. B. "Large, Loving Novel, with Gutsy People." Review of *The Wizard of Loneliness. Nashville Banner* (February 25, 1966).

Tucker, Chris. "Nichols Pours Shot of Wry: Author's Message Lies behind Ironic Wit." *Dallas Morning News* (November 9, 1981).

Ude, Wayne. Review of *On the Mesa. Western American Literature* 22, no. 1 (Spring 1987).

Vigil, Ralph. "The Way West: John Nichols and Historical Reality." *Journal of the West* 24, no. 2 (Kansas State University) (April 1985).

Walker, Hollis. "Activist Nichols Balances Ideology with Success." *Albuquerque Journal* (March 25, 1988).

Walsh, Catherine. "Perspectives: John Nichols." *America* 173, no. 1 (July 1, 1995).

Warga, Wayne. "Unusual Habits of John Nichols." *Los Angeles Times* (October 29, 1981).

Weber, Joan. Review of *An Elegy for September. Library Journal* 117, no. 21 (December 1992).

Weigel, John A. "Fiction Aimed at the Underground." Review of *The Magic Journey. Cincinnati Enquirer* (April 30, 1978).

Welles, Annette. "Delving into a Relationship's Inner Scene." Review of *A Ghost in the Music. Los Angeles Times Book Review* (November 25, 1979).

Whaley, Bill. Review of *Dancing on the Stones. Horse Fly* (February 15, 2000).

Wild, Peter. "John Nichols." *Western Writers Series*, no. 75. Boise, Idaho: Boise State University, 1986.

Wilson, Frank. "An Audacious Triumph in Fiction." Review of *The Nirvana Blues. Fort Worth Star-Telegram* (November 1, 1981).

———. "Nichols Is the Miracle." Review of *The Magic Journey. Philadelphia Inquirer* (May 28, 1978).

———. "The Ribald Tale of a Marriage Made in Hell." Review of *Conjugal Bliss. Philadelphia Inquirer* (February 13, 1994).

Winik, Marian. "Falling to Pieces." Review of *Conjugal Bliss. Washington Post Book World* (February 13, 1994).

Wohlwend, Chris. "Skip Ill-Conceived 'Bliss,' and Live Happily Ever After." Review of *Conjugal Bliss. Atlanta Journal Constitution* (March 6, 1994).

Woodfin, Max. "This Angry Young Man Still Fights Good Fight." *Austin American-Statesman* (January 4, 1983).

Woolf, Jim. "Beauty and Poverty in the Southwest." Review of *A Fragile Beauty. Salt Lake Tribune* (February 7, 1988).

Woolley, Bryan. "A Tribute to the Autumns of Time and Life." Review of *The Last Beautiful Days of Autumn. Dallas Times Herald* (October 3, 1982).

Yakir, Dan. "'Missing' in Action: Costa-Gavras Interviewed by Dan Yakir." *Film Comment* (March/April 1982).

Zoretich, Frank. "John Nichols Novel Reads Like Midlife Journal." Review of *An Elegy for September*. *Albuquerque Journal* (July 26, 1992).

BOOK REVIEWS BY JOHN NICHOLS

Divided Planet: The Ecology of Rich and Poor, by Tom Athanasiou. *Horse Fly* (November 15, 1999).

Blood of the Land: The Government and Corporate War against the American Indian Movement, by Rex Weyler. *Dallas Times Herald* (November 28, 1982).

Teaching a Stone to Talk: Expeditions and Encounters, by Annie Dillard. *Los Angeles Herald Examiner* (November 28, 1982).

Mountain in the Clouds: A Search for the Wild Salmon, by Bruce Brown. *Los Angeles Herald Examiner* (September 19, 1982).

Nuclear Cultures: Living and Working in the World's Largest Atomic Complex, by Paul Loeb. *Dallas Times Herald* (July 11, 1982).

The Bohemians: John Reed and His Friends Who Shook the World, by Alan Cheuse. *Dallas Times Herald* (April 11, 1982).

The Cowboy Cookbook, by Verne Carlson. *Rocky Mountain Magazine* (March 1982).

Witness to Power: The Nixon Years, by John Ehrlichman. *Los Angeles Times* (February 14, 1982).

The Last Texas Hero, by Douglas Terry. *Rocky Mountain Magazine* (January/February 1982).

Cleveland Benjamin's Dead, by Patsy Sims. *Dallas Times Herald* (January 31, 1982).

The Great American Spectaculars, by Jack Ludwig. *Harper's Bookletter* (January 31, 1977).

The Bird Man, by Ian Strange. *Harper's Bookletter* (January 3, 1977).

"Death on the Greasy Grass." Review of four books about The Little Big Horn. *Harper's Bookletter* (October 25, 1976).

The Names: A Memoir, by N. Scott Momaday. *Harper's Bookletter* (December 20, 1976).

ACKNOWLEDGMENTS FOR
"AN AMERICAN CHILD SUPREME"

by John Nichols

I am grateful to these friends for reading my work and offering thoughtful critiques: Emilie Buchwald, Susan Crutchfield, Kathryn Eastburn, Helen Halyard, Alan Howard, Ken Kahn, Ron Kalom, Susan Lang, Maureen McCoy, Tim Nichols, and Scott Slovic.

WORKS CITED

p. x   John Reed, "Almost Thirty," in *Adventures of a Young Man* (San Francisco: City Lights Books, 1975), 142.

p. 5   John Muir, *My First Summer in the Sierra* (Boston: Houghton Mifflin, 1979), 157.

p. 24   Bertolt Brecht, "Praise of Learning," in *Selected Poems,* trans. H. R. Hays (New York: Grove Press, 1959), 93.

pp. 24–25 Nelson Algren, *Chicago: City on the Make* (Sausalito, Calif.: Contact Editions, 1961), 9.

p. 25   Joseph Conrad, *Victory* (Garden City, N.Y.: Doubleday and Company, 1915), 175.

p. 47   Brecht, "To Prosperity," in *Selected Poems,* 173. Copyright © 1947 by Bertolt Brecht and H. R. Hays and renewed 1975 by Stefan S. Brecht and H. R. Hays. Reprinted with permission from Harcourt, Inc.

pp. 56–57 Otto René Castillo, "Apolitical Intellec-
tuals," in *Let's Go!,* trans. Margaret
Randall (Willimantic, Conn.: Curbstone
Press, 1971), 15, 17. English translation
copyright © 1971 by Margaret Randall.
Reprinted with permission from
Curbstone Press.

p. 59 Alan Howard, *New York Times Magazine*
(February 7, 1965).

p. 59 Howard, *New York Times Magazine*
(June 26, 1966).

pp. 60–61 Bernard Malamud, letter to author,
November 4, 1966.

pp. 62–63 John Nichols, from his journal, March 12,
1968.

p. 65 George Jackson, *Blood in My Eye* (New
York: Random House, 1972), 185.

p. 67 Nichols, from his journal, October 13,
1968.

p. 67 Ernesto Che Guevara, *El Socialismo y el
hombre en Cuba* (New York: Pathfinder
Press, 1992), 65. Passage trans. John
Nichols.

p. 71 Nichols, letter to Dave Nichols, April 30,
1967.

p. 72 Nichols, from his journal, May 12, 1969.

pp. 73–74 John Berger, *Art and Revolution: Ernst
Neizvestny and the Role of the Artist in the*

U.S.S.R. (New York: Pantheon Books), 153–54, 157.

pp. 74–75   Nichols, from his journal, October 12, 1968.

p. 76   Nichols, from his journal, October 13, 1968.

p. 88   David B. Morris, *Earth Warrior: Overboard with Paul Watson and the Sea Shepherd Conservation Society* (Golden, Colo.: Fulcrum Publishing, 1995), 100.

p. 91   Walter Lowenfels, *The Revolution Is to Be Human* (New York: International Publishers, 1973), 11.

p. 92   Roque Dalton, *Poetry and Militancy in Latin America* (Willimantic, Conn.: Curbstone Press, 1981), 39. Copyright © 1981 by Curbsone Press. Reprinted with permission from Curbstone Press.

pp. 92–93   Eduardo Galeano, *Open Veins of Latin America: Five Centuries of the Pillage of a Continent,* trans. Cedric Belfrage (New York: Monthly Review Press, 1973), 15.

pp. 93–94   Tom Athanasiou, *Divided Planet: The Ecology of Rich and Poor* (Boston: Little Brown and Company, 1996), 289, 300, 304.

p. 96   Tom Barry, *Guatemala: A Country Guide* (Albuquerque: Inter-Hemispheric Education Resource Center, 1989), 4.

p. 97 Noam Chomsky, introduction to *Bridge of Courage: Life Stories of the Guatemalan Compañeros and Compañeras,* by Jennifer Harbury (Monroe, Maine: Common Courage Press, 1995), 17.

pp. 97–98 Michael Kimmel, *Banished* (unpublished manuscript).

pp. 98–99 Barry, *Guatemala,* 68, 93–4, 120, 123.

p. 100 Chomsky, introduction to *Bridge of Courage,* 27.

p. 105 Barry Commoner, *The Closing Circle: Nature, Man, and Technology* (New York: Alfred A. Knopf, 1971), 292.

p. 105 Jay Mazur, "Globalization's Dark Side," *Foreign Affairs* (January/February 2000): 80.

p. 107 Commoner, *The Closing Circle,* 295.

p. 109 Margaret Randall, *Gathering Rage: The Failure of Twentieth Century Revolutions to Develop a Feminist Agenda* (New York: Monthly Review Press, 1992), 173.

pp. 113–14 Jack Kerouac, *On the Road* (New York: New American Library, 1957), 217.

pp. 114–15 Nichols, letter to Scott Slovic, May 28, 1998.

pp. 118–19 Nichols, *The Milagro Beanfield War* (New York: Ballantine, 1994), 13–14.

pp. 121–22 Nichols, public reading at the Center for Environmental Arts and Humanities, University of Nevada, Reno, November 19, 1998.

p. 122 Nichols, *American Blood* (New York: Henry Holt, 1987), 11.

pp. 122–24 Nichols, University of New Mexico honorary degree speech, Albuquerque, May 13, 2000.

pp. 126–27 Nichols, *Dancing on the Stones* (Albuquerque: University of New Mexico Press, 2000), 176–77.

p. 127 Bruce-Novoa, *Retrospace: Collected Essays on Chicano Literature, Theory and History* (Houston: Arte Publico, 1990), 141.

p. 128 Nichols, "Author's Autobiography," in *Contemporary Authors Autobiography Series,* vol. 2 (Detroit: Gale Research, 1985), 335.

p. 129 Nichols, "To Make a Long Story Short," in *Francis Ford Coppola's Zoetrope All-Story,* ed. Adrienne Brodeur and Samantha Schnee (San Diego: Harcourt, 2000), 174.

p. 130 Nichols, "To Make a Long Story Short," 170.

p. 130 Nichols, *The Nirvana Blues* (New York: Ballantine, 1983), 10.

p. 131 Nichols, *The Nirvana Blues,* 595.

p. 132   Nichols, *The Sky's the Limit: A Defense of the Earth* (New York: W. W. Norton, 1990).

p. 139   Henry David Thoreau, *Walden* (Princeton: Princeton University Press, 1971), 91.

SCOTT SLOVIC, founding president of the Association for the Study of Literature and Environment (ASLE), currently serves as editor of the journal *ISLE: Interdisciplinary Studies in Literature and Environment.* He is the author of *Seeking Awareness in American Nature Writing: Henry Thoreau, Annie Dillard, Edward Abbey, Wendell Berry, Barry Lopez* (University of Utah Press, 1992); his edited and coedited books include *Being in the World: An Environmental Reader for Writers* (Macmillan, 1993), *Reading the Earth: New Directions in the Study of Literature and the Environment* (University of Idaho Press, 1998), *Literature and the Environment: A Reader on Nature and Culture* (Addison Wesley Longman, 1999), and *Getting Over the Color Green: Contemporary Environmental Literature of the Southwest* (University of Arizona Press, 2001). Currently he is an associate professor of English and the director of the Center for Environmental Arts and Humanities at the University of Nevada, Reno.

A Sense of the Morning:
Field Notes of a Born Observer
David Brendan Hopes

Taking Care:
Thoughts on Storytelling and Belief
William Kittredge

This Incomparable Land:
A Guide to American Nature Writing
Thomas J. Lyon

A Wing in the Door:
Life with a Red-Tailed Hawk
Peri Phillips McQuay

The Barn at the End of the World:
The Apprenticeship of a Quaker, Buddhist Shepherd
Mary Rose O'Reilley

Walking the High Ridge:
Life As Field Trip
Robert Michael Pyle

Ecology of a Cracker Childhood
Janisse Ray

The Dream of the Marsh Wren:
Writing As Reciprocal Creation
Pattiann Rogers

The Country of Language
Scott Russell Sanders

Of Landscape and Longing:
Finding a Home at the Water's Edge
Carolyn Servid

The Book of the Tongass
Edited by Carolyn Servid and Donald Snow

Homestead
Annick Smith

Testimony:
Writers of the West Speak On Behalf of Utah Wilderness
Compiled by Stephen Trimble and
Terry Tempest Williams

Shaped by Wind and Water:
Reflections of a Naturalist
Ann Haymond Zwinger

OTHER BOOKS OF INTEREST TO
THE WORLD AS HOME READER

Essays

Eccentric Islands:
Travels Real and Imaginary
Bill Holm

The Heart Can Be Filled Anywhere on Earth
Bill Holm

Shedding Life:
Disease, Politics, and Other Human Conditions
Miroslav Holub

Children's Novels

Tides
V. M. Caldwell

No Place
Kay Haugaard

The Monkey Thief
Aileen Kilgore Henderson

Treasure of Panther Peak
Aileen Kilgore Henderson

The Dog with Golden Eyes
Frances Wilbur

Children's Anthologies

Stories from Where We Live—
The Great North American Prairie
Edited by Sara St. Antoine

Stories from Where We Live—
The North Atlantic Coast
Edited by Sara St. Antoine

Anthologies

Sacred Ground:
Writings about Home
Edited by Barbara Bonner

Urban Nature:
Poems about Wildlife in the City
Edited by Laure-Anne Bosselaar

Verse and Universe:
Poems about Science and Mathematics
Edited by Kurt Brown

Poetry

Turning Over the Earth
Ralph Black

Boxelder Bug Variations
Bill Holm

Butterfly Effect
Harry Humes

Firekeeper:
New and Selected Poems
Pattiann Rogers

Song of the World Becoming:
New and Collected Poems
1981–2001
Pattiann Rogers

THE WORLD AS HOME, the nonfiction publishing program of Milkweed Editions, is dedicated to exploring our relationship to the natural world. Not espousing any particular environmentalist or political agenda, these books are a forum for distinctive literary writing that not only alerts the reader to vital issues but offers personal testimonies to living harmoniously with other species in urban, rural, and wilderness communities.

MILKWEED EDITIONS publishes with the intention of making a humane impact on society, in the belief that literature is a transformative art uniquely able to convey the essential experiences of the human heart and spirit. To that end, Milkweed publishes distinctive voices of literary merit in handsomely designed, visually dynamic books, exploring the ethical, cultural, and esthetic issues that free societies need continually to address. Milkweed Editions is a not-for-profit press.

JOIN US

Milkweed publishes adult and children's fiction, poetry, and, in its World As Home program, literary nonfiction about the natural world. Milkweed also hosts two websites: www.milkweed.org, where readers can find in-depth information about Milkweed books, authors, and programs, and www.worldashome.org, which is your online resource of books, organizations, and writings that explore ethical, esthetic, and cultural dimensions of our relationship to the natural world.

Since its genesis as *Milkweed Chronicle* in 1979, Milkweed has helped hundreds of emerging writers reach their readers. Thanks to the generosity of foundations and of individuals like you, Milkweed Editions is able to continue its nonprofit mission of publishing books chosen on the basis of literary merit—of how they impact the human heart and spirit—rather than on how they impact the bottom line. That's a miracle that our readers have made possible.

In addition to purchasing Milkweed books, you can join the growing community of Milkweed supporters. Individual contributions of any amount are both meaningful and welcome. Contact us for a Milkweed catalog or log on to www.milkweed.org and click on "About Milkweed," then "Why Join Milkweed," to find out about our donor program, or simply call (800) 520-6455 and ask about becoming one of Milkweed's contributors. As a nonprofit press, Milkweed belongs to you, the community. Milkweed's board, its staff, and especially the authors whose careers you help launch thank you for reading our books and supporting our mission in any way you can.

Typeset in Stone Serif
by Stanton Publication Services, Inc.
Printed on acid-free, recycled
55# Frasier Miami Book Natural paper
by Friesen Corporation.